Rabindranath Tagore
Images of Women

Rabindranath Tagore

Images of Women

Selected Poems

Translated by
Jadu Saha

SHIPRA

ISBN: 81-7541-196-1

First Published in India in 2004

11 Weatherwood Cresc.,
Ottawa, ON K2E 7C5, Canada

Published by:
SHIPRA PUBLICATIONS
115-A, Vikas Marg, Shakarpur,
Delhi-110092 (India)
Ph: 22458662, 22500954 Fax: 91-11-22458662
Email : info@shiprapublications.com
www.shiprapublications.com

Laser Typeset by:
Sunshine Graphics
Delhi-110032

Printed at:
Chaudhary Offset Process
Delhi-110051

Dedicated to

Srabani Saha,
Uma Dutta

and

Bharati Chatterjee

Acknowledgements

I sincerely thank my friend, Ruth Latta, for her meticulous editing of the manuscript. Her thoughtful suggestions have improved the flow and other poetical attributes of this translation. Ms. Indrani Sinha of New Delhi has made many helpful suggestions to bring the translations closer to the original poems in Bengali. She has also made many valuable suggestions regarding the English translation. I am indebted to her painstaking editing of both the transliterated versions of the poems and the translated poems.

Contents

Introduction

I

Rabindranath Tagore (1861-1941) was the only literary figure among the twenty most influential Asians of the twentieth century in the *Time* magazine poll in 1999[1]. Though his works in prose are voluminous he is known, not only in his native land of India but also around the world, as a poet. That is, of course, because of his Nobel Prize[2] winning book of poems, *Gitanjali,* and its overflowing praise by William Butler Yeats. In his introduction to *Gitanjali,* Yeats wrote that the poems of Rabindranath Tagore "have stirred my blood as nothing has for years .... I have carried the manuscript of these translations about with me for days, reading it in railway trains, or on the top of omnibuses and in restaurants, and I have often had to close it lest some stranger would see how much it moved me." Alas, this kind of enthusiasm by Yeats and others like Ezra Pound, Wilfred Owen, T. Sturge Moore, Juan Ramón Jiménez, Leonard Woolf, Anna Akhmatova, Hart Crane and Robert Frost did not last long in the English speaking world. To this day, however, Tagore remains an important literary presence in Europe and in the Spanish speaking countries due to translations of his early works from English by great literary figures like André Gide (into French), Juan Ramón Jiménez (into Spanish) and Anna Akhmatova (into Russian). In the English speaking world there were no comparable translators of Tagore in

1. *Time* (Asian Edition), August 1999.
2. Tagore was awarded the Nobel Prize for literature in 1913.

much of the twentieth century. More importantly, Tagore was stereotyped in the Anglophone world as a mystical poet, partly because *Gitanjali* concentrated mainly on his deeply theistic and spiritual poems. American poetry, on the other hand, has generally nothing to do with abstractions, particularly those having to do with spiritual concepts.

Rabindranath's life-long poetical literary output includes about 2500 songs, both lyrics and music and an endless variety of outstanding and innovative varieties of poems, plays in verse and half a dozen musical ballets. His other literary works include three volumes of short stories, novels, plays in prose, essays on a wide variety of subjects, memoirs and personal letters of great literary value. Even more than sixty years after the poet's death only a fraction of his works, including poems, have been translated into English. In recent years a new generation of translators have taken up the challenge of representing Rabindranath to the Anglophone world with a number of excellent translations from the original Bengali. William Radice, Ketaki Kushari Dyson, Krishna Dutta, and Andrew Robinson started this new effort in 1980s and 1990s. Most recent entries in the field in the new millennium are Joe Winters, Wendy Barker and Saranindranath Tagore and *The Oxford Tagore Translations*, edited by Sukanta Chaudhuri. For the sake of completeness, my two previous translations should be added to the list[3].

II

One of the reasons for the sparseness of translations of Tagore's works is the difficulty of translation itself. Translation of poetry is the most difficult of all challenges. The English language simply does not have the equivalents of many concepts basic to Indian thought and many words or phrases commonly used in Bengali. For example, the word sādhanā is a commonly used concept. My Bengali to English dictionary gives its English translation as "austere endeavor; austere

3. *Songs of Rabindranath Tagore* (November, 2002) and *The Flute, Selected Poems of Rabindranath Tagore* (January, 2003). Both published by Shipra Publications, New Delhi.

ascetic practice; worship of God, ..." None of these has the same nuance as the three syllable word sādhanā in Bengali. The same word has different meanings and conjures different images in different contexts in Bengali, as in sangit sādhanā, Bhārater sādhanā. It would give a misleading meaning if these were translated as "austere ascetic practice or worship of God to learn music" or "India's (the country's) austere ascetic practice." In certain contexts "arduous endeavor" or "quest" or "striving" may be the available choices but are not very close in nuance. Another frequently used word is *sudhā,* literally meaning "nectar". It is a noun and is commonly used with another noun in Bengali as in sudhābāri in poem number 9, page 53. Many nuances are in this double noun where one noun, *sudhā* is used to qualify another noun. In this context, the water is not merely sweet (as opposed to salty), satisfying not merely thirst but desire and has the hint of something supernatural about it. In Indian myths, sudhā is the ambrosia, the drink of the gods. In desperation I have used "the water the gods drink." It is a poor approximation.

The difference in language and culture is also demonstrated in mundane matters like clothing and the way it is worn. In Tagore's time, not only village women but also urban women used to pull a part of their sari to partly cover their faces and the Bengali word for it is ghomtā. And when the face is more or less covered the word would be abagunṭhan. The closest approximation is the word 'veil' in English and it is used in reference to weddings. But there is a haunting and charming quality about young women walking along the rural paths, their faces not visible while the tinkling of their bangles and whispers are audible. One could write an essay or even a poem about this image but a one-word translation of ghomtā or abgunṭhan is impossible. In the poem "Requital" I have used the phrase "sari pulled over head" for ghomṭā to indicate when the face is partly covered and veil for abagunṭhan. There are many more difficulties like this in the two languages and cultures.

No translation of poetry from one language to another can bring out the richness, rhythm and the subtleties of the original. Approximate translation is generally considered the best way of making available the poetic riches of one language to those who do not know it. Literal translation, aiming at fidelity to the original text, may transmit ideas and linguistic forms of the original. But its readability is impaired and it fails to convey the mood, tone and meaning behind the words. A literary translation is far better for conveying the flavour, the feel and the meaning apart from being accurate and readable, provided it can stand on its own as literature. Poetry obviously requires literary translation. However, Rabindranath himself was not true to the text of his original poems in Bengali in many of his translations. Sometimes, he even left out, a major portion of a poem and spliced a few lines from one poem with few lines from another to create a new poem. But that is a liberty only the author can take with his own work and not something a translator can do.

Poetry writing has changed considerably in style and content in every language and culture since the end of the Romantic period. Rhymed poetry is now most often found in jingles and Halmark greeting cards and it is rare in literature. Rabindranath was at home with rhyme and, with the exception of four books, all his other poetry was in rhyme. I grew up with Rabindranath's poetry and memorised it. My personal preference is rhymed poetry. In my two previous books of translations of Rabindranath's songs and poems, I maintained the same end rhymes as those of the original. Admittedly, in some instances, the flow was impaired and they sounded like translations. In translating the poems in this book I abandoned rhyme and translated them in free verse.

At the outset I knew I didn't have a prayer of recreating the musical and linguistics of Rabindranath's nuanced and fluid Bengali. Rabindranath was a lyric poet. The flow of his poems has an abundance of rushes of rhythm and playfulness with words. His language is musical, resonant and layered. His choice of words and their arrangement is so precise that replacing one word with a synonym would impair one of these elements. Much of Rabindranath's genius depends on the texture and sound of his poems. How could one render them into another language as dissimilar as English is to Bengali? Instead, I aimed to make the English translations stand on their own merit to please or move the reader. I hope they do.

I have tried to keep as close as possible to the original poems in

Bengali. I have worked through each poem word for word, often to keep the tone or its ambiguities. Also I have tried to keep Rabindranath's syntactical order, with necessary changes in phrasing. I have tried to keep the tone and mood of the poems in "The Runaway", "Postscript", "Satire", "The One who is Dark", and "Last Writings" by using ordinary American colloquial diction. These poems, unlike much of the poet's earlier works are unadorned, informal, compact, direct and written for most part in free verse. They often draw upon the poet's experience in rural Bengal, particularly the time he spent on the Padma while looking after his family estate. In a few instances I have rearranged a few lines but only when the sense of the poem would be lost if the original order was retained. Also, sometimes line breaks have been changed. This has been done to maintain smooth flow.

I have followed standard practices in the use of diacritics in transliteration of the poems in Bengali, with some minor changes where a better known spelling is available. The letters *ri* has been used instead of ṛ.. So instead of Kṛṣṇa it is Kriṣṇa. A key to the diacritics used is given at the end of the book. I have not used any diacritics for the Bengali words retained in the English translations and I have used the spelling commonly used by the Bengalis. These words, unfamiliar to the readers in the West, are marked with a superscript and their meanings are given in the notes at the end.

III

Rabindranath is known outside Bengal mainly as the poet of *Gitanjali* and has been stereotyped in the West as a mystic poet for the theistic and deeply spiritual poems in *Gitanjali* and similar poems published a little later. Even in Bengal his songs are more popular than his poems. Yet the bulk of his poetry was neither his songs nor his 'mystical poems'.

In all his thoughts and works Rabindranath tried to give expression to his innermost emotions and personal experience. Whatever in this world touched his heart he gave expression to it, not by analytical reasoning or from any particular ideology, but from his inner feelings. It is this artistic and skilful expression of personal experience and emotion that is the hallmark of Rabindranath's poetry.

The principal driving force of Rabindranath's poetry was its humanism. No Indian poet since Kalidas in the fourth century A. D. wrote so much about Man and Nature. English poetry is mainly concerned with mankind and Nature whereas Indian poetry is primarily about devotion to God. That is why English poetry has so much variety and complexity. Indian poetry is deep and intensely focused within.

In this respect, Kalidas and Rabindranath are close to the western mind and surprisingly divergent from the main flow of Indian poetry. But western readers see him as a mystic, unlike themselves and the poets of their tradition because they know him only as the poet of *Gitanjali*, in which he wrote about spiritual matters and about his Lord, friend and beloved. They did not have access to the poet's major poetical works, most of which he wrote after *Gitanjali*.

From his childhood Rabindranath dearly loved this 'beautiful world'. Wordsworth found the essence of Creation in Nature and Rabindranath found the essence of Man in Nature. He realised that the beauty of the world is not as perfect and as pure as a hundred-petal lotus. As this realisation crystallised and became deep, his love for the world took a different form, which may be termed as 'hardened'. But there was never a hair-thin crack in it and he never turned his face from mankind and Nature.

Rabindranath tried to build the edifice of his poetry with diverse elements. Alas, it remained incomplete at the time of his death after sixty years of tireless effort. We can say that the poems published until 1914 are 'romantic' and 'sweet'. It is true that many poems of this period reflect detachment, sadness and even bitterness. But the change in his poems, from "The Wild Geese" in 1916 to his death in 1941, is quite remarkable. Rabindranath has called this period his initiation to 'the tune of scorching sun', meaning writing about the unpleasant things in the world. During this period he paid his greatest homage to mankind, not to Nature and not even to his God.

Rabindranath's brilliance was not limited to his literary works or even to painting and sketching, which he started at the age of seventy. He was also an active participant and leader in social and political affairs. When the British divided Bengal into East and West Bengal in 1905 Rabindranath jumped into the protest movement with both feet. But he retired from active participation in politics when the movement turned violent and he became disenchanted with its leadership. He never hesitated to act on his beliefs. Rabindranath renounced his knighthood in 1919 as a protest against the slaughter of 379 innocent men, women and children in Amritsar by the British General, Dyer.

Rabindranath's father, Devendranath, was one of the leaders of *Brahmo Samaj*, a Hindu reform movement started by Raja Rammohan Roy. It was a movement based on the monotheism of the Upanishads, rejection of polytheism, idolatry, the externalised and ritualistic worships of the mainstream Hindus and above all the caste system. Rabindranath left the *Brahmo Mandir* (temple) in his early twenties but up to the end of his life he remained loyal to Rammohan and his legacy. Rabindranath did not follow any particular religion, any path, "ism" or any tradition or social custom blindly. He always walked the path illuminated by the light of his heart. He was critical, even in his poems, of all types of injustice, tyranny and oppression. He was a humanist at all times.

IV

In the selected poems in this book I present one aspect of Rabindranath's humanism — images of women in his poetry. While reading these poems one must keep in mind that the movement of women's liberation and the phrase "gender equality" was not in the English vocabulary when these poems were written. Nor did women had the right to vote in Canada, Switzerland and many other 'first world countries'.

In the selection of poems presented here we will mostly hear Rabindranath's voice speaking about women in the first phase of his poetry up to 1914. In the second phase we will hear mostly women's voice, muted in a man's world, but finding expression in Rabindranath's poems.

The first poem in this selection is from *Manashi* (She who is in the Mind), published in 1890, early in Rabindranth's poetic career. The language and emotion are not quite under control and mature. We hear a woman's voice speaking about love, whose intensity has declined with time, a common experience. The poem's value is not so much in its subject matter as it is in its form and sound. It is lyrical, the principal trait of Rabindranath's poetry all through his life.

The two poems from "The Multicoloured" *(Chitra)* have a common thread running through them. The poet's sense of unity of woman and nature is apparent in many poems in this book. Also apparent are the adorned language, the rush of rhythm and the emotion of human love and love of beauty. In the poem "In the Night and in the Morning", we see the poet's adoration of woman as a lover in the moonlit night and the same woman adored as a goddess in the morning.

> *"In the night you came to my heart*
> *as the beloved, sweetheart,*
> *in the morning, I don't know when*
> *like a goddess you have risen*
> *before me, smiling."* (p. 27)

In "Urbashi," we find the poet adoring woman's enchanting beauty, detached from human relations and need. Urbashi is the embodiment of beauty, enchantment and charm. Her glory radiates from the ancient past to the present and into the future. The memory of hymns in her praise sung by poets and sages in ages past is associated with her. She is the eternal symbol of love and thirst for beauty in man's heart. But she is beyond the reach of man's embrace. The beauty of the poem is in the poet's choice of words, richness of imagery and the overall enchantment. One example will be sufficient:

> *"When you dance in the gods' assembly hall with glee*
> *O swaying, billowing Urbashi!*
> *With that rhythm dances the ocean's surf.*
> *On the heads of crops shivers the earth's scarf.*

The stars fall on sky's floor from the necklace on your breast,
All on a sudden within man's breast his heart knows no rest.
The stream of blood dances in his veins.
Suddenly in the horizon snaps your girdle from its domain,
O you without any restraint." (p. 29)

Rabindranath's adoration of woman continues in the three poems from "Chaitra Harvest", and one poem from each of "Dedication" and "The Wild Geese." In the poem no. 23 of "The Wild Geese" the poet sees woman as the one to whom "flows man's desire", as enchanting as the heavenly nymph, Urbashi and also as Lakshmi, the goddess of human welfare. It is a theme similar to the two aspects of woman we have already seen "In the Night and in the Morning" poem.

The poem "Requital" in this selection is from the book "Stories" *(Katha)* published in 1900. Rabindranath used the book, *The Sanskrit Buddhist Literature of Nepal* (1882) by Rajendralal Mitra as the source material for many poems in "Stories". He wrote two other versions of the same basic story. One was published as a dance drama under the same title and another, a musical ballet with the title, *Shyama*, in 1939. There are some differnces between this poem and the more popular musical ballet, which developed the three principal characters in more details. The essential story seems quite plausible even today judging by the criminal stories published in newspapers. The Shyama depicted in the Buddhist story was a hearlot who discardeded her lovers as frequently and as easily as her beautiful dresses. But the Shyama in Rabindranath's poem is a different woman and from a different time. She is ravishing like the heavenly nymph, Urbashi. But she is lovelorn and falls in love at first sight with Bajrasen whom she sees as "more handsome than the great Indra and appearing high born." Then she commited the "most heinous crime" of her life by entreating the lovesick "adolescent boy, Uttiya," to sacrifice his life to save Bajrasen's life. Here Shyama is shown as not loving Uttiya at all. She is of "stony heart" and selfish in relation to Uttiya and he becomes a martyr for his love for Shyama. But Shyama also sacrificed a lot. She sacrificed all her honour, the king's favours, her fame and fortune as the most adored woman in the kingdom and "severing all ties" she sailed with the lord of her heart and the lord of her "life and death." But Bajrasen could not forgive her for the crime she had committed. All her beseeching was in vain. In the end Shyama lost her love along with everything she had and

> *"gently walked into the forest, as after*
> *awakening from sleep the incomparable dream*
> *of moments before melts into the night's darkness."* (p. 51)

We cannot be as unforgiving as Bajrasen for Shyama's crime and our hearts feel compassion for her than for any other character in the poem.

In the poem "The Strong" in *Indian Butter Tree* we hear the strong voice of a self-assured woman with pride in her womanhood, demanding her rights as man's equal. Here the woman in Rabindranth's imagination is not benumbed in her love for a man. Nor is she dependent on man or thinking of herself inferior to man in any way or a supplicant to him for his love. She does not have the "poverty of submissiveness". She is confident that she has something ineffable in her heart for her beloved. A similar woman's voice appears in the last poem in this selection when the princess Chitrangada declares to the mighty Arjuna of the *Mahabharata* epic:

> *"I am not a goddess nor am I an ordinary woman.*
> *I am not to be worshipped on a pedestal*
> *Nor pushed behind in disrespect.*
> *You will know me*
> *If you keep me by your side in distress and in happiness."*
> (p. 131)

She is man's equal.

Rabindranath held his own progressive views about social issues and problems. He had his independent views about religion too. None of the prevailing relegions really touched his heart, though the theistic interpretation of the Upanishads underpins much of his work, both in prose and in poetry. He always expressed in his writings what he believed to be true. He fearlessly and forcefully spoke against what he believed to be unjust. In many cases his views were opposed to the beliefs, customs and traditions of the Hindu society (as we shall see in his poems). Such fierce independence of opinion regarding religion and social issues was of course, not tolerated and he faced severe opposition from the establishment, including some well known political leaders of his time, such as the great Bipin Chandra Pal. The freedom movement, *swadeshi,* raised a patriotic fervour in the country. Gradually this new-born patriotism turned into an extreme form of conservative nationalism. All types of arguments, including the scriptures, were used to justify everything that was Indian, whether good or bad. Many Indians, educated and illiterate, leaders and followers alike supported the unsupportable without much thought or reasoning. They proved that the habitual inactivity of the people of India was in fact *sattva*[4], the highest quality; idleness was detachment, poverty was riches and self-denial was self-satisfaction.

The great rebel poet of Bengal, Kazi Nazrul Islam, wrote in one poem:

> "Hey dāridra tumi more korecha mahān,
> Tumi more dāniyācha khrisṭer samman."
> "Poverty, you have made me great
> You have given me the same honour as the Christ."
>
> —Translation by the author.

Nazrul perhaps took the literal meaning of Jesus' Sermon on the Mount in which he said, "Blessed are the poor, for theirs is the kingdom of heaven." Jesus was talking about "poverty" of the spirit, absence of egotism and not economic poverty.

Rabindranth, of course did not share such absurd views. So he had no shortage of severe critics of his views expressed in his literary works. The two poems from *The Runway,* "Emancipation" and "Deliverance" and "The Flute Player" from *Shyamali* are

---

4. In the Hindu thought human nature has three basic qualities or tendencies — *sattva,* the primal quality of goodness or virtuousness, *rajas* (unrest, activity) and *tamas* (inertia, dullness).

Rabindranath's scathing condemnation of Hindu practices of cast system, child marriage, and treatment of widows and women in general. The voices of women, muted by men through the ages, find expression in these poems.

The poet had created a new style in rhymed Bengali poetry in *The Wild Geese* where the lengths of the stanzas in a poem are different and so are the lengths of lines. The language was bold and adorned with the choice of words and their arrangements expressing the poet's passion and emotion, and the subject was mainly the issues and problems facing humanity.

In *The Runway* the same style of poetry is there but in a new form. The form is unadorned. Everyday words are arranged in simple fashion, easy flowing, clear and direct. The poems in many cases tell a story, with storytelling more important than poetic form. We see poetry in sudden flashes of similes and metaphors here and there, in the hints of images and scattered sentences with deep meaning.

Rabindranath's deep sympathy and compassion in the face of pain and suffering are another trait in these poems. The poet had more than his share of pain and suffering in his personal life. He could rise above them in his poetry. But he looked at human suffering with sympathy and compassion as made evident in these poems. He created the context and the environment in few lines. None of the poems are burdened with excessive description. The pain and suffering of women in a man's world are depicted in stripped language in a few words, directly and forcefully. Sometimes wit and satire are used to describe injustice and the absurdity of beliefs and social conditions.

Shaila's pain is the subject of the poem *Indelible Mark.* The preference for sons over daughters is common among the people of India even today. Even the mother feels guilty for giving birth to a female child.

"After three daughters, one after the other,
when Shaila came into her father's household
her mother was abashed. ....
It was like a hailstorm
When the farmer wants the rainfall." (p. 59)

What could better describe the stigma of being born as a woman? It certainly is not universal in India today but not rare either. "Shaila started her life with the offence of being innocent." Her mother called her the *unfortunate* and her father berated her as a *curse.* What could be more painful to a little girl? The grandfatherly neighbour was her only friend. The poet's compassion, even for the father, a victim of his own prejudice, comes out at the end when the father cries out after Shaila's tragic death:

> "" *... all that is left is*
> *the indelible mark of*
> *the scribbles of a child's hand on my heart's core.* (p. 63)

Men living in a joint-family in India do not usually notice the extent to which they disregard women, whose lives are "burdened with the wishes of all." This is the subject matter of the poem "Emancipation." In the twenty-two years of married life of the nameless woman, "in a monotonous way the wheel of toil has been grinding away." She "only knew, eating was after cooking and again cooking was after eating." From her deathbed her muted voice finds expression to vent the waste of her life as a woman and even as a human:

> *"When did I have the time*
> *even to think of my pleasure or pain?*
> *Whether this life is good, bad or whatever!*
> *When could I understand that or think of the past or future!"* (p. 65)

She finds a glimmer of hope of fulfilment of her womanhood:

> *"For the first time in my life after twenty-two years*
> *the spring has come into my room.*
> ....
> *I am a woman, I am glorious,*
> ....
> *Without me vain would be the burst of the evening stars*
> *and vain would be the blooming of flowers.* (p. 67)

She finds solace and hope in death, the ultimate equaliser:

"Sweet is the world, sweet I am, a woman,
sweet is death , my eternal supplicant.
Open, please open the door,
take me from the wasted twenty-two years to Time's other shore."
(p. 69)

Has the status of most women in many countries of the world changed much even today? Even in those countries where gender equality is guaranteed by law, there are women "chained to the wheel" of housework, making babies and raising them. Alas, there are women who do all these and hold down a job outside the home.

In India it was not uncommon in Rabindranath's time and it is not uncommon in orthodox Hindu families even now to see a middle-aged or even an elderly man re-marrying while there is a young widowed daughter in the house. The same right was denied to a woman. (It has been changed by law.) Rabindranath has skilfully and vividly exposed the pain and disgrace of womanhood in "*Deliverance*." The double standards of man, the father, and his use of scriptures to defend the chastity of the seventeen-year old widowed daughter for the rest of her life and the righteousness of widowed man is exposed in scathing satire. The poet does not stop exposing the sham of it. He goes further:

" .... When he returned
Home with his wife at last
Manjulika was not home. He learnt from a letter —
Pulin had left with her
For Farakkabad after their marriage
To settle there.
In his anger's rage
The father cursed them time and again." (p. 87)

We find a little satisfaction to see that Manjulika finally had the courage to give a taste of the pain she had suffered day after day at her father's hand. This was the only way and this was the law of nature.

We again hear the woman's voice in "The Flute Player." The voice is of a Bengali woman. The Creator did not give enough time to make her a complete person and left her half done. So there is no harmony between what she is and what she wants to be and her desire is not matched by her will and she is ever unfulfilled. She does not have the guts to even bend the barriers of taboo. She can't love with all her strength. She knows only to shed tears and submit to the will of the society. The flute player is her muse, her deliverer to a fulfilled womanhood. The message of the flute player makes her head rise high in pride and her life seems like the rising sun coming out tearing the curtain of fog and her fervour spreads its wings defying disapproval.

The poem is written in free verse but its language is adorned, lyrical and full of similes:

"Your tune brings in my blood—
The rumble of storm, the surge of flood, the roar of fire,
The assault of the ocean of death
On the rib-cage,
The stirring of the door-chain by the listless wind.
It brings through the narrow channel of unfulfilment
The boom of high tide's plunder
As if to snatch and sweep me away. (p. 121)

The two poems from *Postscript*, "*Basket of Shredded Papers*" and "*Ordinary Woman*" are written in the same style as those in *The Runway.* The language is stripped, direct and conversational. In the "*Basket of Shredded Papers*" we see Amal, a young man, and Sunrita, a young woman falling in love and preparing to get married, disregarding parents' consent and caste barriers. Sunrita is bold and ready to hurt her loving father by leaving his home but Amal backs down in the face of his father's disapproval. The story is told in few words and all descriptions are cut to the bare bones. After four years Amal discovers in Sunrita's abandoned room the shredded love letters, that had been written by him, in a wastepaper basket along with his shredded photograph. These were the only remains of their shattered dream. Also there were two dry flowers as the symbol of their love that had dried up in the heat of caste pride and taboos.

The "*Ordinary Woman*" is a story told by an ordinary woman. The language is conversational, witty and satirical. The young woman is requesting "Saratbabu" to write a story about an ordinary Bengali woman with ordinary hopes and aspirations. Saratbabu is none other than Saratchandra Chattopadhayay (1876-1937), the best loved fiction writer (mostly novels) of Bengal in his time. He was fifteen years younger than Rabindranath but a contemporary. In many of his novels Saratchandra made woman's pain and suffering in a man's world as self-sacrifice and a virtue. Rabindranth is mocking him for this and also mocking himself for his overflowing praise of woman's beauty:

> *"He quoted a few lines from a poem of a Bengali poet*
> *Where Urbashi, the heavenly nymph, rises from the ocean."*
>
> (p. 103)

The reference is to the poet's own poem "*Urbashi*" in this selection discussed earlier. Perhaps Rabindranath's decision to mock his own poem shows that his attitude towards women had changed since he wrote '*Urbashi*" in 1896. He has grown in knowledge and understanding and has realised that praising a woman's beauty does not help her second class status in society.

The poem, "Modern Woman" in *Satire* is written in a light-hearted manner as a satire. The poet is sincere when he says woman is the Muse for his poetry, "raising waves in the heart and awakening songs." He ridicules the term "modern", as any time in history is "modern" compared to previous time. The poet also pokes fun at his critics and at himself. Underneath the satire the poet's high esteem for women is unmistakable.

Again we find Rabindranath's adoration for women in poem no. 23 of *Recovery*, written in the last year of his life. This is his last look at the earth of clay and the humanity he loved so much. He sees the woman as the nurturer of life and the "goddess of life's preservation" like the mother earth. There is also sadness in the poet at the treatment woman receives from man:

> *"Ever aggrieved you are by ingratitude*
> *you bear it all with fortitude."* (p. 127)

The poet pays his homage to woman in this way:

"The duty of the creator
you bear on your shoulder.
You are woman,
you are his companion." (p. 127)

In the last poem of his life, written about a week before his death, in poem no. 15 of *Last Writings* we find the poet paying his last homage to humanity and calling the 'Creator' an enchantress. Woman is not the "Companion" of the Creator but she is herself responsible for the Creation:

"Strewn with a net of diverse deception
is the path of your creation,
O you enchantress" (p. 129)

I am not aware if any other poet or a writer, who has ever been so generous in singing the glory of woman and womanhood.

V

Admittedly, this selection of poems is only a part of Rabindranath's poems about women. In his short stories, in particular, he has written about women eloquently and forcefully as he did in some of his essays. I have presented primarily Rabindranath's poems on women where the poet himself is the speaker and where we hear the voice of women. "*Requital*" can be called a study in the psychology of *one* woman, Shyama.

If these translations can interest readers in exploring further the treasures of Rabindranath's poetry, in translation or the original, that will be my greatest reward.

Ottawa, Canada **Jadu Saha**
March 15, 2003.

Manasi (1890)

Narir Ukti

Miche tarka—thāk tabe thāk.
Kena kāṁdi bujhite pāra nā?
Tarkete bujhibe tā ki? Ei muchilām āṁkhi—
E śudhu cokher jal, e nahe bhartsanā.

Āmi ki ceyechi pāye dhare
Oi taba āṁkhi tule cāoyā,
Oi kathā, oi hāsi, oi kāche āsāāsi,
Alak dulāye diye hese cale ẏāoyā?

Kena āno basantaniśithe
Āṁkhibharā ābeś bihbal
Ẏadi basanter śeṣe śrantamane mlān hese
Kātare khuṁjite hay bidāyer chal?

Āchi ẏena sonār khāṁcāy
Ekkhāni poṣmānā prāṇ.
Eo ki bojhāte hay prem ẏadi nāhi ray
Hāsiye sohāg karā sudhu apaman.

Mane āche sei ek din
Pratham praṇay se takhan.
Bimal śaratkāl, śubhra kṣina meghajāl,
Mridu śitabāye snigdha rabir kiran.

Kānane phuṭita śephālikā,
Phule cheye yeta tarumūl.
Paripūrṇa suradhuni, kulukulu dhbani śuni,
Parapāre taruśreṇi kuāśāākul.

She who is in the Mind (1890)

Woman's Statement

Useless squabble — let's forget it.
Don't you understand why I cry?
Will you grasp it by arguing? Now I am drying my eyes.
It is only my tears and not meant as reproach.

Did I beseech you
to behold me with your eyes,
talk to me, smile, come to me,
or pass me by with a smile, waving your hair?

In spring-night why engender my
eyes with overwhelming rapture
if at the end of spring with a tired mind and sullied smile
you seek hard for an excuse to bid farewell?

As if I am your pet
in a golden cage.
Do I have to explain when there is no love
it is an insult to make one smile with amorous caress?

I remember the time
of the dawn of our love.
It was clear autumn, lace-work of light white clouds
and sunshine in the gentle cool breeze.

In the garden, the *shephalika* was in full bloom
and the ground carpeted with its flowers.
Music was in the murmuring Ganges, full to the brim,
and the trees on the far bank heavy with mist.

Āmāpāne cāhiye, tomār
Āmkhite kāmpita prāṇkhāni.
Ānande biṣade meśā sei nayaner neśā
Tumi to jānonā tāhā, āmi tāhā jani.

Se ki mane paṛibe tomār
Sahasra loker mājhkhāne
Yemani dekhite more kon akarṣandore
Āpani āsite kāche jñāne ki ajñāne.

Kṣanik birahāabasāne
Nibiṛ milañbyākulatā.
Mājhe mājhe sab pheli rahite nayan meli,
Amkhite śunite yena hridayer kathā.

Kono kathā nā rahile tabu
Śudhāite nikaṭe āsiyā.
Nīṛabe caraṇ phele cupicupi kāche ele
Kemane jānite pete, phirite hāsiyā.

Āj tumi dekheo dekho nā,
Sab kathā śunite nā pāo.
Kāche āsa āśā ka're āchi sārādin dhare,
Anmane pāś diye tumi cale yāo.

Dīp jbele dīrgha chāyā laye
Base āchi sandhyāy kajanā
Hayto bā kāche esa, hayto bā dure basa,
Se sakali icchāhīn daiber ghaṭanā.

Ekhan hayeche bahu kāj,
Satata rayecha anyamane.
Sarbatra chilām āmi ekhan esechi nāmi
Hridayer prāntadeśe kṣudra grihakoṇe.

Beholding me, your being
used to quiver in your eyes.
Intoxication in those eyes, joy and sadness mixed—
you don't know them, I do.

Can you remember how
in the midst of millions,
as you sighted me you were drawn by some force,
by some allure's pull, known or unknown?

There was a fervent yearning for union
at the end of each little separation.
At times you used to be swept away and gaze at me
as if you could listen to my heart with your eyes.

Even if there was nothing to say,
you would come to me for the sake saying something.
If I came with silent steps,
somehow you knew it, and turned with a smile.

These days you don't even notice when you see me.
You don't listen to all of what I say.
I wait all day long hoping that you will come to me,
but absentmindedly you pass me by.

In the evening when a few of us are sitting
with the lamp casting a long shadow,
you sometime come near and sit afar —
unwilled chance happenings — all these are.

Now you have much work
and your thoughts are far away.
Once everything to you, I've been left behind
at the edge of your heart, in a small domestic corner.

Diyechile hriday yakhan
  Peyechile prānman deha
Āj se hriday nāi, ȳatai sohāg pāi
  Sudhu tāi abiśbās biṣād sandeha.

Jībaner basante ȳāhāre
  Bhālobesechile ekdin,
Hāy hāy kī kugraha, āj tāre anugraha
  Miṣṭakathā dibe tāre goṭā duītin.

Apabitra o karapaś
  Saṅge or hriday nahile.
Mane ki karecha baṁdhu, o hāsi etai madhu
  Prem nā dileo cale, śudhu hāsi dile.

Tumii to dekhāle āmāy
  (Sbapneo chilo nā eta āśā)
Preme dey katakhāni kon hāsi kon baṇī,
  Hriday bāsite pāre kato bhālobāsā.

Tomāri se bhālobāsā diye
  Bujhechi āji e bhālobāsā
Āji ei driṣṭi hāsi, e ādar rāśi rāśi,
  Ei dūre cale ȳāoā, ei kāche āsā.

Buk pheṭe kena aśru paṛe
  Tabuo ki bujhite pāra nā?
Tarkete bujhibe ta ki? Ei muchilām āṁkhi
  E śudhu cokher jal, e nahe bhartsanā.

✿✿✿✿✿

When you gave me your heart
you had my heart, body and soul.
Today I don't have your heart, no matter how much you caress me,
I have only disbelief, sadness and doubt.

In the spring of your life
the one you loved once—
alas, what a fate! now you pity her
and say only a sweet word or two.

Impure is the touch
if the heart is not there.
Do you think, my love, your smile is so sweet
that is it enough without love?

You, yourself showed me—
(I didn't even hope for so much in my dream.)
How much love can give—what joy, what import—-
how much the heart can love?

With that love of yours
I understand your love of today—
the looks, the smile, the shower of caresses,
this coming near and moving afar.

Even now can't you fathom
why tears rain from my shattered heart?
Will you grasp it by arguing? Now I am drying my eyes.
It is only my tears and not meant as reproach.

✿✿✿✿✿

Citrā (1896)

Rātre O Prabhāte

Kāli madhuyāminīte jyotsnāniśīthe
Kuñjakānane sukhe
Phenilocchal youbansurā
Dharechi tomār mukhe.
Tumi ceye mor āṁkhi'pare
Dhīre pātra layecha kare,
Hese kariyācha pān cumbanbharā
Saras bimbādhare,
Kāli madhuyaminite jyotsnāniśīthe
Madhur ābeśbhare.
Taba abaguṇṭhankhāni
Āmi khule phelechinu ṭāni,
Āmi keṛe rekhechinu bakṣe tomār
kamalkomal pāni
Bhābe nimilita taba yugal nayan,
Mukhe nāhi chila bāṇī.
Āmi śithil kariyā pāś
Khule diyechinu keśarāś,
Taba ānamita mukhkhāni
Sukhe thuyechinu buke āni
Tumi sakal sohāg sayechile, sakhī,
Hāsi mukulita mukhe
Kāli madhuyāminite jyotsnaniśīthe
Nabīnmilansukhe.

Āji nirmalbāy śānta ūṣāy
Nirjan nadītīre
Snān-abasāne śubhrabasanā
Caliyācha dhīre dhīre.
Tumi bām kare laye sāji
Kata tulicha puṣparāji,

The Multicoloured (1896)

In the Night and in the Morning

Yesterday in the honeyed night, in the moonlight,
happily in the bower,
I held the overflowing wine of youth
to your lips.
Beholding my eyes,
gently you took the chalice in your hand,
smilingly you drank it with your ruby lips,
wet with kisses.
Yesterday in the honeyed night, in the moonlight
in the rapture of sweetness
your veil
I snatched away,
your soft hands I pressed
upon my chest —
in ecstasy half closed were your two eyes.
No words were on your lips.
I untied your plait,
unfurled your tresses,
your abashed face
happily on my chest did I place —
You, my beloved, did bear all my amorous caresses
with smiles blossoming on your face,
yesterday in the honeyed night, in the moonlight,
in tender union's happiness.

Today in the clean breeze, in the serene morning
on the solitary river-bank,
just bathed, you are draped
in white and walking slowly.
Basket in left hand
you're gathering heaps of flowers.

Dūrededebālāytale ūṣār rāgiṇī
Bāṁśite uṭhiche bāji
Ei nirmalbāy śānta uṣāy
Jahnabītīre āji.
Debi, taba siṁthimūle lekhā
Naba aruṇsiṁdurrekhā,
Tababām bāhu beṛi śaṅkhabalay
Taruṇ indulekhā.
E kī mangalmayī mūrati bikāśi
Prabhāte ditecha dekhā.
Rāte preyasīr rūp dhari
Tumi esecha prānesbarī,
Prāte kakhan debīr beśe
Tumi samukhe udile hese—
Āmi sambhrambhare rayechi damṛāye
Dūre abanataśire
Āji nirmalbāy śānta uṣāy
Nirjannadītīre.

❁❁❁

Urbaśī

Naha mātā, naha kanyā naha badhū sundari rupasī,
He nandanabāsinī urbaśī.
Goṣṭhe ỹabe sandhyā nāme śrānta dehe sbārnāncala ṭāni
Tumi kona griha prānte nāhi jbālo sandhyādīpakhāni,
Dbidhāy jaṛita pade kamprabakṣe namranetrapāte
Smitahāsye nāhi cala salajjita bāsaraśajyāte
Stabhda ardharāte.
Uṣār uday sama anabagunthitā
Tumi akuṇṭhitā.

Far away in the temple plays the flute
the morning-tune
in the clean breeze, in the serene morning
on the banks of the Ganges in this dawn.
Goddess, on the parting of your hair is drawn
the new sun's vermilion-red line,
encircling your left hand is the conch-shell bangle
like the new moon's sign.
Blossoming in what an auspicious form
you have appeared this morning!
In the night you came to my heart
as the beloved, sweetheart.
In the morning, it seems
like a goddess you have risen
before me, smiling.
In adoration, afar I am standing
with bowed head
in this clean breeze, in the serene morning
on the solitary river's bank.

❀❀❀

Urbashi

Not mother, nor daughter, nor a wife you are to be,
O paradise dweller, ravishing Urbashi.
When on the meadow does the evening descend
Draping round your tired shape with garment's golden end
In any home the evening lamp you do not light;
With faltering steps, trembling heart and downcast sight,
Smiling and blushing to the bridal bed you do not pass
In midnight's hush.
Unveiled as the rise of dawn
Unashamedly you adorn.

Brintahīn puspasama apanate āpani bikaśi
Kabe tumi phuṭile urbaśī.
Ādim basantaprāte uṭhechile manthita sāgare
Dān hāte sudhāpātra biṣabhāṇḍa laye bāmkare,
Tarangita mahāsindhu mantraśānta bhujaṅger mato
Paṛechila padaprānte ucchvasita phaṇā lakṣa śata
Kari abanata.
Kundaśubhra nagnakanti surendrabanditā
Tumi aninditā.

Konokāle chile nā ki mukulikā balikā bayasī
He anantaȳoubanā urbaśī.
Āṁdhār pāthārtale kār ghare basiyā ekelā
Mānik mukutā laye karechile śaiśaber khelā,
Maṇidīpadīpta kakṣe samudrer kallolsaṁgīte
Akalanka hāsya mukhe prabāl pālaṅke ghumāite
Kār aṅkaṭite.
Ȳakhani jāgile biśbe, ȳoubane gaṭhitā
Purṇaprasphuṭitā.

Ȳugȳugāntar hate tumi śudhu bisber preyasī
He apūrba śobhanā urbaśī.
Munigaṇ dhyān bhāṅi dey pade tapasyār phal,
Tomāri kaṭākṣaghāte tribhuban ȳoubancañcal,
Tomār madir gandha andhabayu bahe cāribhite,
Madhumatta bhṛngasama mugdha kabi phire lubdhacite
Uddām saṁgīte.
Nupur guñjari ȳāo ākul–añcalā
Bidyutcañcalā.

Surasabhātale ȳabe nritya kara pulake ullasi
He bilolhillol urbaśī,
Chande chande nāci uṭhe sindhumājhe taranger dal,
Śasyaśīrṣe śihariā kāṁpi uṭhe dharār añcal,
Taba stanahār hate nabhastale khasi paṛe tārā—
Akasmāt puruṣer bakṣomājhe citta ātmahārā,

Blooming like a flower without a stem and free,
When did you blossom, Urbashi?
In the primal spring-morn, out of the *churned sea* you did stand
With the nectar cup in your right, the poison cup in left hand.
The wave-tossed mighty ocean, like a spellbound serpent
With its million heaving hoods bowed at your feet silent.
White as the jasmine undraped resplendence!
The lord of the gods bows in reverence.
O you unblemished radiance!

Were you never tender in age like a maiden budding,
O Urbashi, of youth never-ending?
In ocean's dark vault, sitting lone in whose abode
Did you play childhood games with pearls and gems' load?
In a chamber lit by gems' light, to the billowy song of the sea,
With unblemished smiling face, on a coral-cradle, in whose arms it be
That sleepeth thee?
The moment you woke up in this creation
You were in youth's full-bloom fashion.

From aeons past you're the beloved of all on this earth's face,
O Urbashi, of incomparable grace.
Saints break their meditation to offer their merit of penance.
Youth stirs in the three worlds, struck by the shaft of your glance.
The blind wind blows your intoxicating fragrance all round.
Like a drunken honeybee the poet roams spellbound
With impetuous melody's sound.
Jingling your anklets you go, your garment's end fluttering,
Fast as the lightning.

When you dance in the gods' assembly hall with glee,
O swaying, billowing Urbashi !
With that rhythm dances the ocean's surf.
On the heads of crops shivers the earth's scarf.
The stars fall on sky's floor from the necklace on your breast,
All of a sudden within man's breast his heart knows no rest.

Nāce raktadhārā.
Digante mekhalā taba ṭuṭe acambite
Ayi asambrite.

Sbarger udayācale mūrtimatī tumi he ūṣasī,
He bhubanamohinī urbaśī.
Jagater aśrudhāre dhauta taba tanur tanima,
Triloker hṛdirakte āṁkā taba caranaśoṇimā.
Muktabeṇī bibasane, bikaśita biśbabāsanār
Arabinda–mājhkhāne pādapadma rekhecha tomār
Ati laghubhār—
Akhil mānasasbarge anantaraṅgiṇī,
He svapnasaṅginī.

Oi śuna diśe diśe tomā lāgi kāṁdiche krandasī
He nisṭhurā badhirā urbaśī.
Ādiȳug purātan e jagate phiribe ki ār,
Atal akūl hate siktakeśe uṭhibe ābār?
Pratham se tanukhāni dekhā dibe pratham prabhāte,
Sarbāṅga kāṁdibe taba nikhiler nayan āghāte
Bāribindupāte—
Akasmat mahambudhi apūrba saṁgite
Rabe taraṅgite.

Phiribe nā, phiribe nā— asta geche se gaurabśaśī,
Astacalabāsinī urbaśī.
Tāi āji dharātale basanter ānanda–ucchbāse
Kār cirabiraher dīrghasbās miśe bahe āse,
Pūrṇimāniśīthe ȳabe daśa dike paripūrṇa hāsi
Durasmriti kothā hate bājāy byākul karā bāṁśi—
Jhare aśrurāsi.
Tabu āśā jege thāke prāṇer krandane
Ayi abandhane.

❁❁❁❁❁

The stream of blood dances in his veins.
Suddenly in the horizon snaps your girdle from its domain,
O you without any restrain.

On heaven's crest of sunrise you're embodied dawn glowing,
O Urbashi, you world-beguiling!
The tears of the world wash your slender form.
Your feet, the glow from creation's heart-blood adorn.
With your tresses unbound, form bare,
On the open lotus of the world's desire
You made the seat for your lotus feet
Ever so light!
In all minds' heaven endless is your delight,
O you mate of the dreams of night!

Hark! Around heaven and earth all are crying for thee,
O cruel, heedless Urbashi!
Will the pristine and ancient age come back to the earth again?
From the boundless deep wet-tressed, will you once more rise then?
Will that form first appear in that first morn?
Hurt by the world's eyes, all your limbs will mourn,
Dripping water from your lovely form.
All of a sudden the great ocean will heave and roar
To a song unsung before.

Never again, never again! That moon of glory has set,
O Urbashi, dwelling in eternal sunset.
On the earth today, the burst of joy of the spring
Is mingled with whose deep sigh of eternal parting!
When laughter is all around in the night of the full moon,
From where does the distant memory play its distraught tune?
The tears flow streaming.
Still hope keeps awake in the heart weeping,
O you without bonding!

❀❀❀❀❀

Caitāli (1896)

Mānasī

Śudhu bidhātār sriṣṭi naha tumi nārī
Puruṣ gaṛeche tore soundarȳa sañcāri
Āpan antar hate. Basi kabigan
Sonār upamāsūtre buniche basan.
Saṁpiyā tomār 'pare nūtan mahimā
Amar kareche śilpī tomār pratimā.
Kata barṇa kata gandha bhūṣaṇ katānā,
Sindhu hate mukta āse khani hate sonā,
Basanter ban hate āse puṣpabhār,
Caraṇ rāṅāte kīṭ dey prāṇ tār.
Lajjā diye, sajjā diye, diye ābaraṇ,
Tomāre durlabh kari kareche gopan.
Paṛeche tomār 'pare pradipta bāsanā,
Ardhek mānabī tumi ardhek kalpanā.

✿✿✿

Naṛī

Tumi e maner sriṣṭi, tāi manomājhe
Eman sahaje taba pratimā birāje.
Ȳakhan tomāre heri jagater tīre
Mane hay man hate esecha bāhire.
Ȳakhan tomāre dekhi manomājhkhāne
Mane hay janmājanma ācha e parāne.
Manasīrūpiṇī tumi, tāi diśe diśe
Sakal soundraȳasāthe ȳāo mile miśe.
Candre taba mukhasobhā, mukhe candroday,
Nikhiler sāthe taba nitya binimay.

Chaitra Harvest (1896)

Fancied by the mind

Woman, you're not only God's creation —
man also fashioned you with the fascination
from his heart. The poets weave your attire
with the golden threads of simile. Endowing
you with new charm and grace the artists make
your image eternal. Endless is your colour,
fragrance and raiment— Pearls come from the
depth of ocean and gold from the earth's bosom.
Bevy of flowers comes from spring's treasure
and the bees die to give your feet's colour.
With modesty, with adornment and with veil
you have been cloaked and made hard to attain.
To you flows man's burning desire —
half woman and half fancy you are.

❀❀❀

Woman

You are the creation of my mind. So
your image easily shines in my mind.
When I see you in the world, it seems
that you have appeared from my mind.
When I see you in my mind, I think that
life after life you have been in my heart.
You are mirror of my mind, for everywhere
in all that is beautiful, reflected you are.
The grace of your face is in the moon,
the moon rises in your face —

Maner ananta triṣṇā mare biśba ghuri
Miśāy tomār sāthe nikil madhurī.
Tār pare mangaṛā debatāre, man
Ihakāl parakāl kare samarpaṇ.

❁❁❁

Priyā

Śatabār dhik āji āmāre, sundari,
Tomāre herite cāhi eta kṣudra kari.
Tomār mahimājyoti taba murti hate
Amār antare paṛi chaṛāy jagate.
Ȳakhan tomār 'pare paṛeni nayan
Jagatlakṣir dekhā pāi ni takhan.
Sbarger añjan tumi mākhāile cokhe,
Tumi more rekhe gecha ananta e loke.
E nīl ākaś eta lagita ki bhālo,
Ȳadi nā paṛita mukhe taba mukhāālo.
Aparūp māyābale taba hāsigān
Biśbamājhe labhiyāche śata śata prāṇ.
Tumi ele āge āge dīp laye kare,
Taba pāche pāche biśba paśila antare.

❁❁❁❁❁

forever is this exchange with the world.
Mind's infinite thirst, suffusing you
with all charms, dies roving the universe.
At last, man offers his life here and after
to the goddess of his mind's construct.

❀❀❀

Beloved

Shame, a million shames on me, O you beautiful!
for wanting to see you as a miniature.
The splendour from your form shining on my heart
showers on the world.
When my eyes were not on you,
I didn't see the goddess of world's splendour.
Giving my eyes the blush of heaven,
you have left me in this endless world.
If my mind didn't reflect your radiant face,
the blue sky would not be so enchanting.
Your laughter and song, in some exquisite
magic, come alive in millions of forms.
You came first, lamp in hand and then
the world followed into my heart.

❀❀❀❀❀

Katha (1900)

Pariśodh

'Rājkoṣ hate curi Dhare ān cor,
Nahile nagarpal, rakṣā nāhi tor
Munda rahibe nā dehe' Rājār śāsane
Rakṣidal pathe pathe bhabane bhabane
Cor khumje khumje phire. Nagarbāhire
Chila śuye bajrasen bidirṇa mandire
Bideśi banik pāntha takṣaśilābasi;
Aśba becibār tare esechila kaśi,
Dasyuhaste khoāiyā niḥsba rikta śeṣe
Phiriyā calitechila āpanār deśe
Niraśbāse—tāhāre dharila cor bali.
Haste pade bamdhi tār lohār śikali
Laiyā calila bandiśāle.

Sei kṣane
Sundaripradhānā śyāmā basi bātāyane
Prahar jāpitechila ālasye koutuke
Pather prabāha heri; nayansammukhe
Sbapnasama lokyātrā. Sahasā śihari
Kampiyā kahila śyāmā, 'Aha mari mari
Mahendraninditakānti unnatadarśan
Kāre bandi kare āne corer matan
Kaṭhin śrinkhale Śighra yā lo sahacari
Bal ge nagarpāle mor nāṃ kari,
Śyāmā dākiteche tāre; bandi sāthe laye
Ek bār āse yena e kṣudra ālaye
Dayā kari' Śyāmār nāmer mantraguṇe
Utalā nagarrakṣi āmantran śune
Romāncita; satbar paśila grihamājhe,

Stories (1900)

Requital

"Burglary in king's treasury! Catch the burglar,
otherwise, the Police Chief you're in danger,
your head will not be on your shoulders!"
With the king's decree the police, out in force,
searched all streets and every door. Outside the city
sleeping in a decrepit temple was Bajrasen,
a travelling foreign merchant from *Takshila*.
He came to *Kashi* to sell horses but losing
his all to a band of brigands was at last
returning home — penniless and hopeless.
The police arrested him as the thief. He was
being taken to the prison with hands and feet
tied in iron chains.

At that time,
Shyama, first among the most beautiful, was
seated by the window idling away her time
in jest, watching the traffic flow. Right before her
eyes was a parade of people, as if in a dream.
Shuddering in a sudden shock, Shayama cried out,
"Oh my God, oh God! More handsome looking
than the great *Indra* and appearing high-born—
Whom they are taking like a thief in chains of iron!
Run, my friend, be quick and tell the policeman
that Shyama begs his presence and if he would
please bring the prisoner to my humble abode."
With the magic of Shyama's name the policeman,
beside himself with excitement at the request,
at once came into the house with Bajrasen,

Piche bandi bajrasen nataśir lāje
Āraktakapol. Kahe rakṣi hasyabhare,
'Atiśay asamaye abhājan'pare
Aȳācita anugrahā Calechi samprati
Rajkārye. Sudarśane deha anumati.'
Bajrasen tuli śir sahasā kahilā,
'Eki līlā, he sundarī, eki taba līlā
Path hate ghare āni kiser koutuke
Nirdoṣ e prabāsīr abamān dukhe
Karitecha abamān' Śuni śyāmā kahe,
'Hāy go bideśī pantha, koutuk e nahe,
Āmār angete ȳata sbarṇa alaṃkār
Samasta sampiyā diyā śrinkhal tomār
Nite pāri nija dehe; taba apamāne
Mor antarātmā āji apamān māne.'
Eta bali siktapakṣma duṭi cakṣu diyā
Samasta lānchnā ȳena laila muchiyā
Bideśīr anga hate. Kahila rakṣīre
'Āmār ȳā āche laye nirdoṣ bandīre
Mukta kare diye ȳāo.' Kahila praharī,
'Taba anunay āji ṭhelinu sundarī,
Eta e asādhya kāj. Hrita rājkoṣ,
Binā kāro praṇpāte nripatir roṣ
Śānti mānibe nā' Dhari praharīr hāt
Kātare kahila śyāmā, 'Śudhu duṭi rāt
Bandīre bamcāye rekho e minati kari.'
'Rākhiba tomār kathā', kahila praharī.

Dbitīyā rātrir śeṣe khuli bandīśālā
Ramaṇī paśila kakṣe, hāte dīpjbālā,
Lohār śringkhale bāmdhā ȳethā bajrasen
Mrityur prabhāt ceye mouni japichen
Iṣṭanām. Ramanīr kaṭakṣāingite
Rakṣi āsi khuli dila śrinkhal cakite.
Bismaybihbal netre bandi nirakhila
Sei śubhra sukomal kamalunmila

his cheeks red and head bent low. With a smile
the policeman said, "Why this unexpected
favour on this undeserving one at this
inopportune time ? Now I am on royal duty.
Oh beautiful one, please give your command."
All of a sudden, raising his head Bajrasen said,
"What sport is this, oh you beautiful, what jest!
What a joke you're enjoying, calling in an innocent
foreigner from the street to add insult to his pain
of shame." After listening to him Shyama said,
"Alas! Foreign traveller, it is not a joke.
Giving away all gold adornments on my body
I can wear your chains instead. The core of my
being is afflicted with shame at your shame."
So saying with two dewy eyes as if she sponged
all disgrace from his body, she told the policeman,
"Please take all my treasures and let the innocent
prisoner free." The policeman said in response, "Oh
Beautiful, I must spurn your request this time,
for it is such a difficult task. The king's treasure
has been robbed. Without taking someone's life
the king's anger will not be appeased." Taking
the policeman's hands in hers Shyama beseeched,
"Please keep the prisoner alive for only two nights. It is
my plea." "I'll honour your request," said the policeman.

At the end of the second night, opening the prison door
the woman entered, lamp in hand, where Bajrasen
in iron chains was waiting for the dawn of the day
of his death, praying in silence to his deity. The
sentry at once, at a meaningful signal of the woman,
removed the prisoner's chains. With a bewildered
look the prisoner gazed at the incomparable
white-lotus face. He said in an emotion-choked voice,
"At the end of the nightmare of the horrible night

Aparūp mukh. Kahila gadagadasbare,
'Bikārer bibhiṣikārajanīr pare
Karadhritaśuktārā śubhra uṣāsama
Ke tumi udile āsi kārākakṣe mama
Mumurṣur praṇrūpā, muktirūpā ayi,
Niṣṭhur nagarīmajhe lakṣmi dayāmayī'

'Āmi dayāmayī' Ramanīr uccahāse
Cakite uṭhila jāgi naba bhayatrāse
Bhayaṃkar kārāgār. Hāsite hāsite
Unmatta utkaṭ hāsya śokaśrurāśite
Śatadhā paṛila bhāni. Kāṁdiyā kahilā,
'E purīr pathamājhe ȳata āche śilā
Kaṭhin śyāmār mato keha nāhi ār'
Eta bali driṛhabale dhari hasta tār
Bajrasene laye gela kārār bāhire.
Takhan jāgiche uṣā baruṇār tīre,
Pūrba banāntare. Ghāṭe bāṁdhā āche tarī.
'He bideśī, eso eso' kahilā sundarī
dāṁṛāye noukār 'pare, 'He āmār priya,
Śudhu ei kathā mor smaraṇe rākhiyo,
Tomā sāthe ek srote bhāsilām āmi
Sakal bandhan ṭuṭi he hridaysbāmī,
Jībanmaraṇprabhū' Noukā dila khuli.
Dui tīre bane bane gāhe pākhiguli
Ānandāutsabgān. Preyasīr mukh
Duibāhu diyā tuli bhari nija buk
Bajrasen śudhāila, 'kaho more priye,
Āmāre karecha mukta kī sampad diye.
Sampūrṇa jānite cāhi ayi bideśinī,
E dīndaridrajan taba kāche rhiṇī
kata rhiṇe.' Āliṅgan ghanatar kari
'Se kathā ekhan nahe', kahila sundarī.

Noukā bhese cale ȳāy pūrṇabāyubhare
Tūrṇasrotobege. Madhyagaganer 'pare

who are you like the morning star
appeared in my prison cell — life of the dying,
deliverer of the doomed, goddess of benevolence,
embodiment of kindness in this unkind city!"

"Me, embodiment of kindness!" At the woman's
loud laughter awoke the terrible prison in some new
terror's fear. It broke into hundred pieces in wild,
grotesque laughter, drenched in raining tears.
Bemoaning, she said, "No stone in the streets of this city
is as hard as this Shyama!" So saying, taking Bajrasen's
hands in firm grip, she came out of the prison.
The dawn was just awakening on the banks of
the *Baruna* beyond the eastern forests. A boat
was moored there. "Come if you please, oh you stranger,"
said the angelic woman standing in the boat,
"Oh my beloved, bear only this in your mind, that
I sail with you in the same stream, severing all ties for
you, the lord of my heart, the lord of my life and death!"
The boat sailed. The birds were singing merry melodies
in forests of the two shores. Holding his lover's head
with both hands against his chest Bajrasen said,
"Tell me, my beloved, with what treasure did you
buy my freedom? I want to know it all, oh you
stranger, what is the burden of debt of this poor,
hapless one?" Firming her embrace said the
enchantress, "Please, it is not the time."

The boat sailed on in full wind in the fast
flowing current. The blazing sun was above
the head in the midday.The village women,
after baths, had gone home in wet attire carrying
brass pots filled with the Ganges-water. Abandoned

Udila pracanda śurya. Grāmbadhugaṇ
Grihe phire geche kari snān samāpan
Siktabastre kāṃsyaghaṭe laye gaṅgājal.
Bheṅe geche prabhāter hāṭ; kolāhal
Theme geche dui tīre; janapada bāṭ
pānthahīn. Batatale pāṣāṇer ghāṭ,
Sethāy bāṁdhila noukā snānahārtare
Karṇadhār. Tandrāghana baṭaśākhā'pare
Chāyāmagna pakṣinīr gītaśabdahīn.
Alas pataṅga śudhu guñje dirgha din.

Pakkaśasyagandhaharā madhyāhṇer bāye
Śyāmār ghomṭā ȳabe phelila khasāye
Akasmāt, paripūrṇapraṇaypīṛāy
Byathita byākul bakṣa, kaṇṭha ruddhaprāy,
Bajrasen kāne kāne kahila śyāmāre,
'Kṣaṇikśrinkhalmukta kariyā āmāre
Bāṁdhiyācha ananta śrinkhale. Kī kariyā
Sādhilā duḥsādhya brata kaha bibariyā.
Mor lāgi kī karecha jāni ȳadi priye,
Parisodh diba tāhā e jiban diye
Ei mor paṇ.' Bastra ṭāni muk'hpari,
'Se kathā ekhano nahe' kahila sundarī.

Guṭaye sonār pāl sudure nīrabe
Diner āloktarī cali gela ȳabe
Astāacaler ghāṭe, tīrupabane
Lāgila śyāmār noukā sandhyār pabane.
Śukla caturthir candra astagata prāy,
Nistaranga śānta jale sudīrgha rekhāy
Jhikimiki kare kṣīṇ ālo; jhillisbane
Tarumūlandhakār kāmpiche saghane
Bīnār tantrer mato. Pradīp nibāye
Tarībātāyantale dakṣiner bāye
Ghananiśbasitamukhe ȳubaker kāṁdhe
Heliyā baseche śyāmā. Paṛeche abādhe

was the morning-marketplace, silenced was the clamour on both the banks, deserted were the roads. There was a stone *ghat* in the shade of a Banyan tree. The boatman moored the boat there for bathing and a meal. On the tree branches in deep slumber, in shadow's cover, silent were the songs of the birds in their nests. Only the idle crickets chirped in the long day. The wind, laden with the fragrance of ripened harvest, when unveiled Shyama's face all of a sudden, smitten by love's pain and an aching heart Bajrasen asked Shayama in a choked voice, "Unfettering my fleeting chains you have bound me in an eternal chain. Please tell me how you accomplished this impossible task. If I know what you have done for me, my love, I'll pay it back with my life, this is my promise." Pulling her sari over her face said the enchantress — "Not now."

Gathering her golden sail in the silent far away when the day's boat of light went to the sunset shore, Shyama's boat, in the evening wind, anchored in a wooded shore. The moon of the fourth night of the bright fortnight was about to set. The dim light was shimmering on the calm water in long lines; the forest floor was quivering like strings of *veena* with the crickets' chirping. Blowing out the lamp, Shyama, bathed in the south wind and in quickened breath, was reposed on the young man's shoulder by the boat's window. Her unbound, unfettered perfumed tresses, covered the soft

Unmukta sugandha keśarāśi, sukomal
Tarangita tamojāle cheye bakṣatal
Bideśir, sunibiṛ tandrājālsama.
Kahila asphuṭkanṭhe śyāmā, 'Priyatama, veena

Tomā lāgi ȳā karechi kaṭhin se kāj,
Sukaṭhin, tāro ceye sukaṭhin āj
Se kathā tomāre balā. Saṃkṣepe se kaba;
Ekbār śune mātra man hate taba
Se kāhinī muche phelo.—

Balak kiśor
Uttīya tāhār nām, byartha preme mor
Unmatta adhīr. Se āmār anunaye
Taba curīapabād nijaskandhe laye
Diyeche āpan prāṇ. E jibane mama
Sarbādhik pāp mor, ogo sarbottama,
karechi tomār lāgi e mor gourab.'

Kṣīṇ candra asta gela. Araṇya nīrab
Śata śata bihanger supti bahi śire
Daṃṛāye rahila stabdha. Ati dhire dhire
Ramaṇīr kaṭi hate priyabāhudor
Śithil paṛila khase; bicched kaṭhor
Niḥśabde basila doṃhāmājhe; bākyahīn
Bajrasen ceye rahe āṛaṣṭa kaṭhin
Pāṣāṇputtali; māthā rākhi tār pāye
Chinnalatasama śyāmā paṛila luṭāye
Ālingancyutā; masīkrisna nadīnīṛe
Tīrer timirpuñja ghanāila dhīre.

Sahasā ȳubār jānu sabale baṃdhiyā
Bāhupāśe, ārtanarī uṭhila kāṃdiyā
Aśruhārā śuṣkakanṭhe, 'kṣamā karo nath,
E pāper ȳāhā daṇḍa se abhisampāt

breast of the stranger in an enchanting wave of
darkness. Shayama said in a hushed voice,
"My beloved, what I did for you was very difficult.
It is even more difficult for me to tell you now.
I'll be brief. You must erase it from your mind
after hearing the story this once.

An adolescent boy,
Uttiya was his name, was bewildered in his
unrequited love for me. At my entreaty
he sacrificed his life shouldering the burden
of false charge of theft against you. In this
life it is the most heinous sin I've committed, my
most precious. It was my pride that I did it for you."

The faint moon faded. Congealed silence fell upon
the forest. It stood unmoved carrying the burden of
hundreds of feathered creatures on its head. Very slowly
the beloved's arms, twined around the woman's waist,
dropped off. Stony estrangement came between the
two in silence. Speechless Bajrasen's frozen eyes looked
at her like a statue. Shyama, parted from embrace,
sprawled at his feet like a severed vine. The shadows from
the banks slowly gathered on the ink-black river water.

All of a sudden, firmly twining around
the young man's knees, the grieving woman cried out
in a parched voice, "Forgive me, my lord, the punishment

Hok bidhātār hāte nidāruṇtaro
Tomā lāgi yā karechi tumi kṣamā karo.'
Caraṇ kaṛiyā laye cāhi tār pāne
Bajrasen bali uṭhe, 'Āmār e prāṇe
tomār kī kāj chilā E janmer lāgi
Tor pāpmūlye kenā mahāpāpbhāgi
E jiban karili dhikritā Kalankinī,
Dhik e niśbās mor tor kāche rhiṇī
Dhik e nimeṣpāt pratyek nimeṣe.'
Eta bali uṭhila sabale. Niruddeśe
Noukā chaṛi cali gelā tīre, andhakāre
Banamājhe. Śuṣkapatrarāsi padabhāre
Śabda kari araṇyere karila cakita
Pratikṣaṇe. Ghanagulmagandhapuñjikrita
Bāyuśunya banatale tarukānḍaguli
Cāri dike āṁkā baṁkā nānā śākhā tuli
Andhakāre dhariyāche asaṃkhya ākār
Bikrita birūp. Ruddha hala cāri dhār.
Nistabdhaniṣedhsama prasārila kar
Latāśrinkhalita ban. Śrantakalebar
Pathik basila bhume. Ke tār paścāte
Dāṁṛāila upacchāyāsamā Sāthe sāthe
Andhakāre pade pade tāre anusari
Āsiyāche dīrgha path mounī anucarī
Raktasiktapade. Dui muṣṭi baddha kare
Garjila pathik, ''Tabu chāribi nā more'
Ramani bidyutbege chuṭiyā paṛiyā
Banyār tarangāsama dila ābariyā
Ālingane keśapāśe srastabeśabāse
Āghraṇe cumbane sparśe saghana niśbāse
Sarba anga tār; Ardragadagadabacanā
Kanṭharuddhaprāy 'chāriba nā' 'chāriba nā'
Kahe barambār, 'Tomā lāgi pāp, nath,

for this sin — may that curse be more severe at the hands of Providence — but forgive me for the crime I committed for you." Wresting away his feet and gazing at her Bajrasen said, "Of what use was this life to you! Cursed is this life forever bought with my share of the price of your colossal crime! You sinner, shameful is every breath indebted to you! Shame on every look I cast on this world." So saying he got up forcefully and leaving the boat he came aimlessly on land into the forest's darkness. With every step rustling of the dry leaves under his feet startled the forest. In the concentrated smell of the dense shrubs in the airless forest floor the tree trunks, spreading in all directions with zigzag branches made many ugly, grotesque forms in the dark. The woods closed in around him. The forest shackled in vines stretched its arms like a silent barrier. The traveller sat on the ground, his limbs exhausted. Who stood behind him like a shadow's shadow! Along with him in the darkness following his every step came a long way a silent companion with bleeding feet. The traveller with two clenched fists roared, "Won't you leave me alone yet!" In a flash the woman in dishevelled clothing burst upon him like a torrent's waves deluging him with embraces, kisses, caresses, smothering him with her dishevelled tresses. "I won't let you go, I won't," she sobbed again and again in a choked voice. "I've committed this sin for you, my lord, you punish

Tumi śasti dāo more, karo marmāghat,
Śeṣ kare dāo mor daṇḍa puraskār.'
Aranyer grahatārahīn andhakār
Andhabhābe kī yena karila anubhab
Bibhīṣikā. Lakṣa lakṣa tarumul sab
Māṭir bhitare thāki śiharila trāse.
Bārek dhbanila ruddha niṣpeṣita śbāse
Antim kākuti sbar, tāri parakṣaṇe
Ke paṛila bhūmīpare asāṛ patane.

Bajrasen ban hate phirila yakhan
Pratham uṣār kare bidyutbaran
Mandirtriśūlcūṛā jahnabīr pāre.
Janahīn bālutaṭe nadīdhārēdhāre
Kāṭāila dīrgha din kṣipter matan
Udāsīn. Madhyāhṇer jbalanta tapan
Hānila sarbānge tār agnimayi kaśā.
Ghatkakṣe grāmbadhū heri tār daśā
Kahila karuṇ kanṭhe, 'ke go griha chāṛā,
Eso āmāder ghare.' Dila nā se sāṛā.
Triṣṇay phāṭila chāti, tabu sparśila nā
Sammukher nadī hate jal ekkaṇā.
Dinśeṣe jbartapta dagdha kalebare
Chuṭiyā paśila giyā taraṇīr 'pare,
Patanga yeman bege agni dekhe dhāy
Ugra āgraher bhare. Herila śayāy
Ekṭi nūpūr āche paṛi; śatabār
Rākhila bakṣete cāpi. Jhaṃkār tāhār
Śatamukh śarsama lāgila barṣite
Hridayer mājhe. Chila paṛi ek bhite
Nīlāmbar bastrakhāni, rāśikrita kari
Tari 'pare mukh rākhi rahila se paṛiī
Sukumār dehagandha niśbase niḥśeṣe
Laila śoṣaṇ kari atripta ābeśe.
Śukla pañcamīr śaśī astācalgāmī

me, cut me to the quick, and be done with my punishment
or reward !". —Bereft of stars and planets the darkness
of the forest in its blindness sensed some frightful threat.
The roots of millions of trees under the earth shivered
in premonition. For once sounded under a muffled breath
the last supplication and in the next moment
someone fell to the ground — motionless.

When Bajrasen came out of the forest the first ray
of dawn was reflecting on the Ganges the trident
on the temple's crown, bright as lightning. He spent
a long day on the deserted sandy banks like a frenzied,
disinterested man. The scorching midday sun
struck him with lashes of fire. A village woman,
carrying a pitcher, seeing his plight, said in a doleful
tone, "Oh you homeless, please come to our home."
He gave no response. His heart was about to crack
with thirst yet he didn't touch a drop of water
from the river before him. At the end of the day,
his frame burning hot, he ran to the boat
like a moth flying into the fire in fiery
fervour. He found only one anklet lying
on the bed. He pressed it tight to his chest for a
hundred times. Its tinkles, like hundred-headed
arrows, pierced into his heart. Lying there in a
corner was her blue sari. Gathering it he stayed
burying his face — breathing in the fragrance
of her lovely body in unquenched enchantment.
The moon of the fifth night of the bright fortnight
was setting behind the top of the branches of
the *seven-leafed tree.* Stretching his two hands towards

Saptaparṇataruśire paṛiyāche nāmi
Śākhāantaṛāle. Dui bāhu prasariyā
Dākiteche bajrasen, 'eso eso priyā'
Cāhi aranyer pāne. Henakāle tire
Bālutatẹ ghanakriṣña baner timire
Kār murti dekhā dila upacchāyā sama.
'Eso eso priyā' 'āsiyāchi priyatamā'
Caraṇe paṛila śyāmā, ''kṣama more kṣamā
Gela nā to sukaṭhin e parāṇ mama
Tomār karuṇ kare' Śudhu kṣanatare
Bajrasen tākāila tār mukh'pare,
Kṣaṇatare alingan lāgi bāhu meli,
Camaki uṭhila, tāre dūre dila ṭheliī
Garajila, 'kena eli, kena phire eli'
Bakṣa hate nūpūr laiyā dila pheli,
Jbalanta angārsama nilāmbarkhāni
Caraṇer kāch hate phele dila ṭāni;
Śayyā yena agniśayyā, padatale thāki
Lāgila dahite tāre. Mudi dui āṁkhi
Kahila phirāye mukh, 'yāo yāo phire,
More cheṛe cale yāo' Nari nataśire
Kṣaṇatare rahila nirabe. Parakṣaṇe
Bhūtale rākhiyā jānu yubār caraṇe
Praṇamila, tār pare nāmi naditire
Āmdhār baner pathe cali gela dhire,
Nidrābhange kṣaniker apūrba sbapan
Niśār timirmājhe milāy yeman.

the forest called out Bajrasen, "Come, come my beloved!"
Just at that time on the sandy shore, in the deep forest
darkness, appeared a face like the shadow of a shadow.
"Come, come my beloved!" "I have come my dearest!"
Shyama fell at his feet, "Forgive, do forgive me!
This stony heart of mine didn't crumble in your tender
hands!" Only for a moment Bajrasen looked at her face,
for a moment he opened his arms to embrace
and then in utter shock he pushed her aside
thundering, "Why did you come, why did you come back!"
He flung the anklet from the nest of his chest.
He threw the blue sari from near his feet like
burning amber. The bed became flaming fire,
kept on burning him from under his feet. Shutting
his eyes he turned his face, "Go, go back and leave
me alone!" The woman remained silent for a moment,
her head bent low. Next moment she paid her
obeisance kneeling. Then alighting on the riverbank
she gently walked into the forest as after
awakening from sleep the incomparable dream
of moments before melts into the night's darkness.

Utsarga

No. 43

Sānga hayeche raṇ.
Anek ȳujhiyā   Anek khuṁjiā
Śeṣ hala āyojan.
Tumi esa esa nārī,
Āna taba hemjhāri.
Dhuye muche dāo dhūlir cinha,
Joṛā diye dāo bhagnāchinna,
Sundar karo sārthak karo
Puñjita āyojan.
Eso sundari nārī,
Śire laye hemjhāri.

Hāṭe ār nāi keha.
Śeṣ kare khelā   Cheṛe enu melā,
Grāme gaṛilām geha.
Tumi eso eso nārī,
Āno go tīrthabāri.
Snigdhahasita badan indu,
Siṁthāy āṁkiyā siṁdūrbindu
Mangal karo sārthak karo
Śunya e mor geha.
Eso kalyāni nārī,
Bahiyā tīrthabāri.
Belā kata ȳay beṛe.
Keha nāhi cāhe   Khar̄rabidāhe
Parabāsi pathikere.
Tumi eso eso nārī,
Āno taba sudhābāri.

Dedication (1914)

No. 43

The struggle is over.
After a lot of striving, a lot of searching
completed are all preparations.
Come, come, you fair woman,
bring your golden watering can.
Banish the last trace of dust,
bind the broken and torn,
make beautiful and fruitful
all amassed preparations.
Come, come beautiful woman
with the golden watering can on your crown.

There is no one in the market.
ending pleasure, leaving the fair,
I've built my home in the village.
Come, come fair woman,
with water from the holy sites.
With your face smiling like the moon,
adorning the vermilion dot on your hair's parting.
Make auspicious and gratify
my lonesome home.
Come, come auspicious woman
with the water from the holy sites.

The day is fast advancing.
No one cares for a traveller from a foreign land
in this blazing sun.
Come, come fair woman,
bring the water the gods drink.

Bājāo tomar niṣkalanka
Śata-cāṁdēgaṛā śobhan śankha,
Baraṇ kariyā sarthak karo
Parabāsī pathikere.
Ānandamayi nārī,
Āno taba sudhābārī.

Srote ye bhāsila bhelā.
Ebārer mato din hala gata.
Ela bidāyer belā
Tumi eso eso nārī,
Āno go aṣrubāri.
Tomār sajal kātar driṣṭi
Pathe kare dik karuṇabriṣṭi,
Byākul bāhur paraśe dhanya
Hok bidāyer belā
Oyi biṣādinī nārī,
Āno go aśrubāri.

Āṁdhār niśītharāti.
Griha nirjan Śunya śayan,
Jbaliche pūjār bāti.
Tumi eso eso nārī,
Āno tarpaṇbāri,
Abarita kara byathita bakṣa
Kholo hridayer gopan kakṣa,
Elōkeśapāśe śubhrābasane
Jbālāo pūjār bāti.
Esa tapasinī narī,
Āno tarpaṇbāri.

✿✿✿✿✿

Blow your glorious conch-shell
fashioned from a hundred moons.
Make the foreign traveller fulfilled
by welcoming him.
O you joyful woman,
bring the water the gods drink.

Now the raft drifts in the current.
This term has now come to an end
and it's time to bid farewell.
Come, come fair woman
with tears in your eyes.
May your distressed tearful look
shower compassion on my path.
May my parting be blessed
with your ardent arms embrace.
O you doleful woman,
rain your tears.

Dark is the midnight.
The house is desolate, the bed is deserted
and the lamp burns for worship.
Come, come fair woman and
bring the water for oblation.
Unlock the afflicted heart
and open the soul's secret door.
Draped in white, with tresses unbound,
light the lamp of worship.
Come, you ascetic woman,
bring the water for oblation.

✿✿✿✿✿

Balākā

No. 23

Kon kṣane
Srijaner samudramanthane
Uṭhechila dui nārī
Ataler śayātal chāṛī.
Ekjanā urbaśī, sundari,
Bisber kāmanārājye rāni,
Sbarger apsarī.
Anyajanā lakṣmī se kalyāṇī,
Bisber janani tāṁre jāni,
Sbarger Īśbarī.

Ekjan tapobhanga kari
Uccahāsyāagnirase phalguner surāpātra bhari
Niye ȳay prānman hari,
Dūhāte chaṛāy tāre basanter puṣpita pralāpe,
Ragarakta kiṃśuke golāpe,
Nidrāhīn ȳoubaner gāne.
Arjan phirāyā āne
Aśrur śiśir snāne
Snigdha bāsanāy;
Hemanter hemkānta saphal śāntir pūrṇatāy;
Phiriyā āne
Nikhiler āśirbādpāne
Añcal lābanyer smitahāsyasudhāy madhur.
Phirāyā āne dhīre
Jiban mrityur
Pabitra sangamtīrthe
Ananter pūjār mandire.

Wild Geese (1916)

No. 23

At the time of creation
during the churning of the ocean[i],
leaving their bed
from the abysmal depth rose two women.
One was Urbashi[i], the ravishing,
the queen of the realm of desire,
the nymph of the heaven.
The other one was *Lakshmi*, the beneficent.
We know her to be the mother of the universe,
the supreme goddess in heaven.

One, disrupting ascetic practices,
fills the spring's goblet with splendor of laughter.
Plundering the heart and soul she
disperses them in the madness of the flower-burst of spring
in the colours of *kingshuks* and roses
and in the song of sleepless youth.
The other one brings back
calmed longing,
bathed in the dewdrops of tears
in the gratified utmost peace of golden *hemant.*
The charm of calmness bathed in sweet smile,
she gently brings back
to the auspicious confluence
of life and death and
to the Infinite's temple of worship.

✽✽✽✽✽

Palātakā (1918)

Ciradiner Dāgā

Opār hate epār pāne kheyānauko beye
Bhāgya neye
Dale dale ānche chelemeye.
Sabāi samān tārā
Ek sājite bhareānā campāphuler pārā.
Tāhār pare andhakāre
Kon ghare se poumchiye dey kāre
Takhan tāder ārambha hay naba naba kāhinījālbonā—
Duḥkhe sukhe dinmuhūrta gonā.
Eke eke tinṭi meyer pare
Śaila yakhan janmālo tār bāper ghare,
Jananī tār lajjā pela; bhābla kothā theke
Abānchita kānālṭāre ānla ghare deke.
Briṣṭidhārā cāiche yakhan cāṣi
Namla yena śilābriṣṭirāśi.

Binādoṣer aparādhe śailabālār jiban hala śuru,
Pade pade aparādher bojhā hala guru.
Kāraṇ binā ye anādar āpni oṭhe jege
Beṛei cale se yē āpan bege.
Mā tāre kay "poṛārmukhi," śāsan kare bāp,—
E kon abhiśāp
Hatabhāgī ānli baye— śudhu kebal bemce thākār pāp.
Yatai tārā dita ore gāli
Nirmalāre dekhta malin mākhiye tāre āpan kathār kāli.
Nijer maner bikarṭirei śaila orā kay,
Oder śaila bidhir śaila nay.

Āmi briddha chinu oder pratibeśī.
Pāṛāy kebal āmār sange dusṭu meyer chila mesāmeśi.

The Runway (1918)

Indelible Mark

In his ferryboat, from the far-shore to the near
the helmsman, Destiny, brings
bevies of children.
They are all the same
just like the *champak* flowers in a basket.
Who is then delivered to which home
is a mystery.
Then begins the weaving of their novel stories
and marking of days and moments with joy and sorrow.
After three daughters, one after the other,
when *Shaila* came into her father's household
her *mother was abashed.* She thought that she had invited
from somewhere this unwanted and unfortunate one
into her home.
It was like a hailstorm
when the farmer wants the rainfall.

Shaila started her life with the offence of being innocent,
and the load of her offence became heavier with every step.
Disdain, arising without any cause
grew by its own momentum.
Mother called her "the unfortunate" and berated the father —
"What a curse!
You wretch, you came carrying only the sin of being alive.
The more they cursed her the more they made
the blameless one guilty with the smear of their own words.
They named the aberration of their mind *Shaila*, the millstone.
But what was a millstone to them was not to God.

I was just an old man, their neighbour.
The naughty girl was cordial only with me in the neighbourhood.

"Dādā" bale
Galā āmār jaṛiye dhare basta āmār kole.
Nām śudhāle āmāy balta hāsi hāsi.
"Āmār nām ye duṣṭu sarbanāśī"
Ȳakhan tāre sudhātem tār mukhṭi tule dhare
"Āmi ke tor bal dekhi bhāi more?"
Balta "dādā, tui yē āmār bar̃".
Emni kare hāsāhāsi hata paraspar.

Biyer bayas hala tabu konomate hay nā biye tārī
Tāhe bāṛāy aparādher bhār.
Abaśeṣe barmā theke pātra gela juṭi.
Alpadiner chuṭi;
Śubhakarma sere tāṛātāṛi
Meyeṭire sange niye rengune tār dite habe pāṛi.
Śailake yei balte gelem hese.
"Buṛo barke helā kare nabinke bhāi baraṇ karli śeṣe?'
Amni ye tār ducokh gela bhese
Jharjhariye cokher jale. Āmi bali "Chi chi,
Kena, śaila, kaṁdis michimichi,
Karis amangal."
Balte giye cakṣe āmār rākhte nari jal.

Bājla biyer baṁśi,
Anādarer ghar cheṛe hāy bidāy hala duṣṭu sarbanāśī.
Ȳabār belā bale gela, "dādā tomār raila nimantraṇ,
Tiñsatyi—ȳeo ȳeo." "ȳāba, ȳāba, ȳāba bai ki bon."
Ār kichu nā bale
Āśirbāder motir mālā pariye dilem gale.

Caturtha din prāte
Khabar ela, irābatīr sāgarīmohanāte
Oder jāhāj dube geche kiser dhākkā kheye.
Abār bhāgya neye
Śailare tār sange niye kon pāre hāy gela nouko beye
Kena ela kenai gela kei bā tāhā jāne.

Addressing me as *Dada*
she would sit on my lap, her arms around my neck.
If I asked her name, Shaila would smilingly say,
"My name is Naughty Calamity!"
Holding her face up if I would ask,
"Tell me dear, who am I to you?"
She would say, "Dada, you are my beau!"
This is how we laughed together.

She became of marriageable age but marriage didn't happen—
so the load of her guilt grew.
At last a groom from Burma was found.
He had only a few days off and
after the auspicious event
he would have to sail for Rangoon in a hurry.
When I told Shaila in jest,
"Abandoning your old beau at last you welcomed a young one!"
At once her eyes were flooded,
raining tears. I said, "Shame, shame,
Shaila, you are crying for nothing,
it's inauspicious."
To say this I could not hold my tears.

The wedding-flute played.
Alas, Naughty Calamity left forever the home of unwelcome.
Before departing she said, "Dada, you have an open invitation,
scout's honour, you must come." "I'll come, of course I will, sister
dear."
Without saying any more
I adorned her with the pearl necklace of blessing.

On the morning of the fourth day
the news came. After a collision
their ship sank in the confluence of the Irawati and the ocean.
Again the helmsman, Destiny,
carried Shaila in his boat to some unknown shore.

Nimantraṇti rekhe gela śudhu āmār prāṇe.
Ȳāba ȳaba ȳāba, didi, adhik deṛi nāi,
Tiñsatyi āche tomār, sēkathā ki bhulte pāri bhāi.
Āro ekṭi cinha tāhār rekhe geche ghare
Khabar pelām pare.
Gāliye buker byathā
Likhe rākhi eikhāne sei kathā.

Diner pare din cale ȳay, oder bāri ȳai ne āmi ār.
Niye āpan ekla prāner bhār
Apan mane
Thāki āpan koṇe.
Henakāle ekadā mor ghare
Sandhyābelāy bāp ela tār kiser tare.
Balle, "Khuṛo ekṭā katha āche,
Bali tomār kāche.
Śaila ȳakhan choṭo chila, ekadā mor baksa khule dekhi
Hisāblekhā khātār 'pare e ki
Hijibiji kālir āṁcar. Māthāy ȳena paṛla krodher bāj.
Bojhā gela śailari e kāj.
Mārādharā gāli manda kichute tār hay nā kono phal,—
Haṭhat takhan mane ela śastir kouśal.
Mānā kare dilem tāre
Tomār bāṛi ȳāoyā ekebāre.
Sabār ceye kaṭhin danḍa. Cup kare se raila bākyahīn
Bidrohiṇi biṣam krodhe. Abaśeṣe bāro diner din
Garabini garba bheṅe balle ese, 'āmi
Ār kahano karba na duṣṭami.'
Āmcaṙkāṭā sei hisāber khātā,
Sei kakhānā pātā
Ājke āmār mukher pāne ceye āche tāri cokher mato.
Hisāber sei ankagulār samay hala gata;—
Se śāsti nei, se duṣṭu nei;
Raila sudhu ei

Who knows why did she come and why did she go!
Only she left the invitation in my heart.
I'll go, I'll go, my dear sister, without much delay.
I gave you the scout's honour, can I ever forget that my dear?
I came to know of it later
that she had left something of her in her house.
Let me write it down
with the pain in my heart

Days marched on and I didn't go to their house anymore.
With the load of my lonesome heart
I stayed
in my own corner.
After a while her father
came to me for something one evening.
He said, "Uncle, I have something
to tell you.
When Shaila was very young, one day, opening my box,
I found in my book of accounts strange
scribbling in ink. Anger struck me like a thunderbolt.
I knew it was Shaila's doing.
Spanking and scolding had no effect on her.
In a flash a novel punishment came to my mind.
I forbade her
not to come to your house ever.
It was the most severe punishment of all! The rebellious
kept silent in extreme anger. At last after twelve days
the pride of the spirited was broken.
She came to say, 'I'll never be naughty again.'
The scribbles in my book of accounts,
those few pages
stare now at my face as if they are her eyes.
The time is past for the numbers in my account book;
punishment is no more, nor she is naughty anymore;
all that is left is

Ciradiner dāgā
Śiśūhāter āṁcaṛ kaṭi āmār buke lāgā."

❁❁❁

Mukti

Dāktār ẏa bale baluk nāko,
Rakho rakho khule rākho,
Śiyarer oi jānlā duṭo,ī gāye lāguk hāoya.
Oṣudh? Āmār phuriye geche oṣudh khāoā.
Tito karā kata oṣudh khelem e jībane,
Dine dine kṣaṇe kṣaṇe.
Beṁce thākā, sei ẏena ek rog;
Katarakam kabirāji katai muṣṭiẏog
Ekṭu mātra asābdhānei, biṣam karmabhog.
Eiṭe bhālo, oiṭe manda, ẏe ẏā bale sabār kathā mene,
Nāmiye cakṣu, māthāy ghomṭā ṭene,
Bāiś bachar kāṭiye dilem ei tomāder ghare.
Tāi to ghare pare,
Sabāi āmāy balle lakṣmi satī,
Bhālo mānuṣ ati.

E saṃsāre esechilām nābacharer meye,
Tār pare ei paribārer dīrgha gali beye
Daśer icchā bojhāīkarā ei jibantā tene ṭene śeṣe
Pouṁchinu āj pather prānte ese.
Sukher dukher kathā
Ekṭukhāni bhābba eman samay chila kothā.
Ei jībanṭā bhālo, kiṃbā manda, kiṅbā yāha'kekṭā kichu
Se kathāṭā bujhba kakhan, dekhba kakhan bhebe
āgupichu.
Ekṭānā ek klānta sure
Kājer cākā calche ghure ghure.
Bāiś bachar rayechi sei ek-cākātei baṁdhā

the indelible mark of
the scribbles of a child's hand etched on my heart's core."

Emancipation

Let the doctor say whatever he likes.
keep, please keep them open—
the two windows towards my head — let me feel the breeze.
Medicine? I am done with taking medicine.
I have taken the bitter, the acrid — all kinds in this life,
on every day, at every moment.
Staying alive, it seems, is a disease in itself.
Many kinds of Ayurvedic and plain home remedies too—
just a little carelessness and at once bad consequences.
This is good, that is bad — obeying whatever any one said,
with eyes down cast, veiling my face
I spent twenty-two years in your household.
That's why people in and outside the family
say how good I am, how obedient,
indeed, very decent!

I came into this household as a nine-year old girl,
then along the long alley of this family,
dragging my life burdened with the wishes of all,
I've come to the end of my road at last.
When did I have the time
even to think of my pleasure or pain?
Whether this life is good, bad or whatever!
When could I understand that or think of the past or future!
In a monotonous way
the wheel of toil has been grinding away.
I've been tied to that wheel for twenty-two years

Pāker ghore āṁdhā.
Jāni nāi to āmi ȳe kī, jāni nāi e brihat basundharā
Kī arthe ȳe bhara.
Śuni nāi to mānuṣer ki bāṇi
Mahākāler biṇāy bāje. Āmi kebal jāni,
Rāṁdhār pare khāoya, ābār khaoyār pare rāṁdhā,
Bāiś bachar ek-cākātei bāṁdhā.
Mane hacche sei cākāṭā-oi ȳe thāmla ȳena;
Thāmuk tabe. Ābār oṣudh kena.

Basantakāl bāiś bachar esechila baner āninīy.
Gandhe bibhol dakṣiṇ bāy
Diyechila jalsthaler marma-dolāy dol;
Heṁkechila, "Khol re duār khol."
Se ȳe kakhan āsta ȳeta jānte petem nā ȳe.
Hayto maner mājhe
Saṃgopane dita nāṛā; hayto gharer kāje
Acambite bhul ghatāta; hayto bājta buke
Janmāntarer byāthā; kāraṇ-bholā duḥke sukhe
Hayto parān raita ceye ȳena re kār pāyer śabda śune,
Bihbal phālgune.
Tumi āste āpis theke, ȳete sandhyābelāy
Pāṛāy kothā śataranja khelāy.
Thāk sēkatha.
Ājke kena mane āse prāṇer ȳata kṣnik byākulata.
Pratham āmār jībane ei bāiś bachar pare
Basantakāl eseche mor ghare.
Janlā diye ceye ākāś pāne
Ānande āj kṣaṇe kṣaṇe jege uṭhche prāṇe
Āmi nārī, āmi mahīyasī,
Āmār sure sur beṁdheche jyotsnābīṇāy nidrābihīn śaśī.
Ami naile mithyā hata sandhyātārā oṭhā,
Mithyā hata kānane phulphoṭā.

in a dizzying spell.
I didn't know who I was or with what message
this vast world was filled.
I did not hear what message for mankind
sounds in the harp of endless Time. I only knew,
eating was after cooking and again cooking was after eating;
for twenty-two years I was chained to the same wheel.
It seems that the wheel is coming to a stop — let it be—
no more medicine for me.

For twenty-two years the spring came to the forest.
The south-wind, laden with fragrance,
churned the heart of the land and water.
It called out, "Open, open your door."
I never knew when it came and went.
Perhaps secretly it shook
my mind; perhaps suddenly it caused
mistake in my housework; or perhaps my heart
felt the pains of many lives; oblivious to the
causes of pain and pleasure my heart ached in the beguiling
spring days on hearing someone's footsteps.
In the evening on returning from the office, you used to go
somewhere in the neighbourhood to play chess.
Forget those things.
I don't know today why the longings of my heart churn my mind.
For the first time in my life after twenty-two years,
the spring has come into my room.
Looking at the sky through the window
I feel, in every moment, sheer delight springing in my heart —
I am a woman, I am glorious.
My mood pulsates in the moonbeams of the sleepless moon.
Without me, vain would be the burst of the evening stars,
and vain too would be the blooming of flowers.

Bāiś bachar dhare
Mane chila bandi āmi anantakāl tomāder ei ghare.
Duḥkha tabu chila nā tār tare,
Asāṛ mane din keṭeche, āro kaṭta āro bam̐cle pare.
Ȳethāy ȳata gñāti
Lakṣmī bale kare āmāy khyāti;
Ei jībane sei ȳena mor param sārthakatā
Gharer koṇe pam̐cer mukher kathā
Ājke kakhan mor
Kaṭla bām̐dhañdor.
Janam maraṇ ek hayeche oi ȳe akūl birāt mohanāy,
Oi aṭal kothāy mile ȳay
Bhām̐ṛār gharer deyāl ȳata
Ekṭu phenār mato.
Etadine pratham ȳena bāje
Biyer bām̐śi biśba ākāś mājhe.
Tuccha bāiś bachar āmār gharer koṇer dhulāy paṛe thāk.
Marañbāsarghare āmāy ȳe diyeche dāk
Dbāre āmār prārthī se ȳe, nay se kebal prabhu,
Helā āmāy karbe nā se kabhu.
Cāy se āmār kāche
Āmār mājhe gabhīr gopan ȳe sudhāras āche
Grahatārār sabhār mājhkhāne se
Oi ȳe āmār mukhe ceye dām̐ṛiye hothāy raila nirnimeṣe.
Madhur bhuban, madhur āmi nārī,
Madhur maraṇ, ogo āmār ananta bhikhāri.
Dāo, khule dāo dbār,
Byartha bāiś bachar hate pār kare dāo kāler pārābār.

✿✿✿

For twenty-two years I thought that
I was a prisoner in your household for eternity.
Yet there was no remorse for it, years passed
with mind paralysed, more would have passed if I lived longer.
All the relatives everywhere
would have praised me as *Lakshmi*, the good;
as if that is the supreme fulfilment of my life —
the words of their praise though imprisoned in the house!
Sometime today
all my bonds have been severed.
Birth and death has become one in a vast, endless confluence
where the abysmal depth melts somewhere,
as do all the pantry walls —
like a fleck of foam.
After so long, for the first time,
the wedding-flute plays in the vault of the universe.
Let the insignificant twenty two years remain in the dust of my room.
The one, who calls me to my bridal chamber of death,
is longing for me at my door and not merely my master,
he will show never disrespect to me.
He wants from me
the nectar that is in the depth of my heart.
Standing in the assembly of planets and stars
he is gazing at me with unblinking eyes.
Sweet is the world, delightful I am, a woman,
sweet is death, my eternal supplicant.
Open, please open the door,
take me from the wasted twenty-two years to Time's other shore.

❀❀❀

Niṣkriti

Mā keṁde kay, "manjulī mor oi to kaci meye,
Ori saṅge biye debe?—bayase or ceye
Paṁcgun se baṛo;—
Tāke dekhe bāchā āmār bhayei jaṛasaṛo.
Eman biye ghaṭte deba nāko."

Bāp balle, "kannā tomār rākhõ
Pañcananke pāoyā geche anek diner khoṁje,
Jāno nā ki masta kulīn o ẏe.
Samāje to uṭhte habe seṭā ki keu bhāba.
Oke chāṛle pātra kothāy pāba."
Mā balle, "Kena oi ẏe caṭujyeder pulīn,
Nāibā hala kulīn,
Dekhte ẏeman temni sbābhābkhāni
Pās kare pher peyeche jalpāni,
Sonār ṭukro chele.
Ekpāṛāte thāke orāī ori sange hese khele
Meye āmār mānuṣ hala; oke ẏadi bali āmi āji
Ekkhani hay rāji."

Bāp balle, "Thāmo,
Āre āre rāmoḥ.
Orā āche samājer sab talāy.
Bamun ki hay paite dilei galāy?
Dekhte sunte bhālo halei pātra halã Rādhẽ
Strībuddhi ki śāstre bale sādhe."

Ẏedin orā gini diye dekhle kaner mukh
Sedin theke manjulikār buk
Prati paler gopan kāṁṭāy hala rakte mākhā.
Māyer sneha antarẏāmī. Tār kāche to ray nā kichui dhāka;
Māyer byathā meyer byathā calte khete śute
Gharer akāś pratikṣaṇe hānche ẏena bedanābidyute.
Aṭalatār gabhīr garba bāper mane jāge,—

Deliverance

Raining tears the mother said, "Do you want to give in marriage
my Manjuli, such a baby girl? — He is
five times as old.
My baby is scared stiff just looking at him.
Such a marriage will never happen even in my dreams."

The father said, "Your wailing must stop.
A groom like Panchanan I've found after turning over many stones.
The *glory of his lineage* you don't know.
Do you ever think that we have to climb up the social ladder?
Where shall I find such a groom if we let him go!"
The mother said, " Why not Pulin of the Chatterji family?
He may not be of high pedigree —
His nature is as good as his looks,
again he got a scholarship after graduating.
He is such a gem of a son.
He and my daughter grew up playing together in the
same neighbourhood. If I say the word
he will agree at once."

The father said, "Stop right there,
What a disgraceful affair!
They are at bottom rung of the ladder.
Are all birds equal because they have feathers?
For a groom, good looks and good conduct do not make the cut.
Shame! It is not for nothing the scripture says 'woman's thinking'."

From the day the groom's party blessed her with a gold coin,
blood from the jabbing of an invisible thorn
soaked Manjulika's heart.
Mother's love knew it all, nothing remained hidden.
Mother's sorrow, daughter's sorrow at all times
struck the spirit of the house with the lightning of pain.
A great pride of firmness filled the father's heart.

Sukhe duḥkhe dbeṣe rāge
Dharma theke naṛen tini nāi hena dourbalya.
Tāṁr jībaner rather cākā calla
Lohār bāṁdhā rāstā diye pratikṣaṇei,
Konomatei incikhānek edikodik ekṭu habār jo nei.

Tini balen, tāṁr sādhanā baṛoi sukaṭhor,
Ār kichu nay, śudhui maner jor,
Aṣṭābakra jamadagni prabhriti sab rhiṣir saṅge tulya,
Meyemānuṣ bujhbe nā tār mūlya.

Antaḥśilā aśrunadīr nīrab nīre
Duṭi nārīr din baye ȳāy dhire.
Abaśeṣe baiśākhe ek rāte
Manjulikār biye hala pañcānaner sāthe.
Bidāybelā meyeke bāp bale dilen māthāy hasta dhari
"Hao tumi sābitrīr mato ei kāmanā kari."

Kimāścarȳamtaḥpraṃ, bāper sādhañjore
Āśīrbāder pratham aṅśa dūmās ȳetei phalla keman kare—
Pañcānanke dharla ese ȳame;
Kintu meyer kapālkrame
Phalla nā tār śeṣer dikṭā, dile nā ȳam phire,
Manjulikā bāper ghare phire ela siṁdur muche śire.

Duḥkhe sukhe din haye ȳay gata
Sroter jale jhaṛēpaṛā bheseȳāoā phuler mata,
Abaśeṣe hala
Mañjulikār bayas bharā ṣolo.
Kakhan śiśukāle
Hridaȳlatār pātār antarāle
Beṛiyechila ekṭi kuṁṛi
Prāner gopan rahasyatal phuṁṛi;

No weakness he had of bending his innate nature —
may that be in joy, sorrow, malice or anger.
The wheels of the chariot of his life
ran along an iron clad path at all time,
without straying an inch on either side.

He said that his way was very austere indeed.
It was nothing but strong single-mindedness
comparable to *Astabakra*, *Yamadajna* and the other sages.
No woman could appreciate its preciousness.

The two women's time passed slow
in the stream of their secret tears' flow.
At last in one night of *Baishakh*
Manjulika was given in marriage to Panchanan.
At the time of her parting the father blessed his daughter —
"May you be like *Savitri* and it is my prayer."

Surprise of surprises, due to her father's austere practices
within two months the first part of his blessing came to pass.
The god of death got Panchanan;
but due to the destiny of the daughter
the last part didn't happen. The god of death didn't give
him back.
Wiping the vermilion dot from her forehead Manjulika returned
to her father's home.

Time passed in joy and sorrow
like fallen flowers floating in a current.
At long last
Manjulika became full sixteen.
She didn't know
when in childhood
hidden in the heart's bower
a bud did appear

Jānta nā to āpnāke se,
Śudhāy ni tār nām konodin bāhir hate khepā bātās ese,
Sei kuṁṛi āj antare tār uṭhche phuṭe
Madhur rase bhare uṭhe.
Se ȳe premer phul
Āpan rāṅā pāpṛibhāre āpni samākul.

Āpnāke tār cinte ȳe ār nāiko bāki,
Tāito thāki thāki
Camke oṭhe nijer pāne ceye.
Akāśpārer bāṇī tāre dāk diye ȳay ālor jharṇā beye;
Rāter andhakāre
Kon asīmer rodanbharā bedan lāge tāre.
Bāhir hate tār
Ghuce geche sakal alaṃkār;

Antar tār rāṅiye oṭhe stare stare,
Tai dekhe se āpni bhebe mare.
Kakhan kājer phāṁke
Jānlā dhare cup kare se bāire ceye thāke—
Yekhāne oi śajne gācher phuler jhuri beṛār gāye
Rāśi rāśi hāsir ghāye
Ākāśṭāre pāgal kare dibasrāti.

Ȳe chila tār chelebelār khelāgharer sāthi
Āj se keman kare
Jalasthaler hridaykhāni dila bhare.
Arūp haye se ȳena āj sakal rūpe rūpe
Miśiye gela cupe cupe.
Pāyer śabda tāri
Marmarita pātāy pātāy giyeche sañcāri.
Kāne kāne tāri karun bāṇī
Moumāchider pākhār gugunāni.

from the depth of her soul's mystery.
The untamed wind, coming from without, never asked its name.
Filled with sweet nectar
that bud now blossomed in her heart.
It was the flower of love,
bewildered and heavy with its own rosy lips.

She had nothing more to know about herself.
That's why every now and then
looking at herself she startled quite often.
Messages from the sky's domain called her in light's fountain.
In the night's darkness
pain of cries assailed her from some boundless.
Gone was forever
all outward adornment for her.

She was at a loss in despair
to see her heart filling with colour, layer upon layer.
Sometimes in the midst of her work she would stare,
holding on to the window's bars,
at the world where near the fence the flowers' abundance
from the horseradish plant made the sky
intoxicated with their laughter all day and night.

He who had been the playmate of her play-house
in childhood, now somehow
filled her heart at all times.
In all forms that were beautiful he had quietly
dissolved as the formless.
The sound of his footsteps
raised rustles in the leaves.
The humming of the bees
struck her ears as his doleful pleas.

Meyer nīrab mukhe
Kī dekhe mā, śel bāje tār buke.
Nābalā kon gopan kathār māyā
Mañjulikār kālo cokhe ghaniye tole jalbharā ek chāyā;
Aśrūbhejā gabhīr prāner byathā
Ene dila adhare tār śaratniśir stabdha byākulatā.
Māyer mukhe anna roce nāko—
Keṁde bale, "Hāy bhagabān, abhāgīre phele kothāy thāka."

Ekadā bāp dupurbelāy bhojan sānga kare
Guṛguṛiṭār nalṭā mukhe dhare,
Ghumer āge ȳeman cirābhyās,
Paṛtechilen iṃreji ek premer upanyās.
Mā ballen bātās kare gāye,
Kakhano bā hāt buliye pāye,
"Ȳār khuśi se ninde karuk, maruk biṣe jare
Āmi kintu pāri ȳeman kare
Manjulikār debai deba biye."

Bāp ballen kaṭhin hese, "tomrā māye jhiye
Ek lagnei biye karo āmār marār pare,
Sei kaṭā din thāko dhairya dhare."
Ei bale tāṁr guṛguṛite dilen mridu ṭān.
Mā ballen, "uḥ kī pāṣāṇ prāṇ,
Snehamāyā kicchu ki nei ghaṭe.'
Bāp ballen, "āmi pāṣāṇ baṭe.
Dharmer path kaṭhin baṛo, nanir putul hale
Etadine keṁdei jetām gale."

Mā ballen, "Hāy re kapāl. Bojhāi bā kāre.
Tomār e saṃsāre
Bharā bhoger madhyakhāne duār eṃṭe
Pale pale śukiye marbe chāti pheṭe

Sensing something in her
daughter's silent face a bolt hit the mother's heart.
On Manjulika's dark eyes the magic of some
unspoken secret message cast a water-laden shadow.
The pain, steeped in tears, from the depth of her being
imparted on her lips the silent restlessness of autumn evening.
Food became distasteful to mother.
In tears she cried, "My Lord, where have You gone
forsaking this unfortunate one?"

One day the father after his midday feast,
while smoking his *hookah*
as usual, was reading
an English romance just before his nap.
The mother said, fanning him at times
and caressing his feet sometimes,
"Let them slander if they prefer,
Let them stew in their juice, but I promise
I'll again give Manjulika in marriage somehow."

The father said, cracking a stony smile, "Both of you,
mother and daughter, can marry at the same time
after I'm gone, but have patience until then."
So saying he took a gentle drag of his hookah.
The mother said, "Oh what a stony heart
without any tenderness or affection in any part!"
The father said, "Stony heart indeed!
The path of righteousness is very hard indeed! If I were
a butter-doll I would have melted by now
in the scorching heat of sorrow."

The mother said, "What a pity! How shall I explain?
In your household
in the midst of plenty and behind a closed door,
so young a girl will shrivel to death of heartache —

Eklā kebal ekṭuku oi meye,
Tribhubane adharma ār nei kichu er ceye.
Tomār puṁthir śukno pātāy nei to kothāo prāṇ,
Darad kothāy bāje seṭā antarȳamī jānen bhagabān."

Bāp ekṭu hāsla kebal, bhāble, "meyemānuṣ
Hridaytāper bhāpēbharā phānus.
Jiban ekṭā kaṭhin sādhan—nei se oder jñān."
Ei bale pher calla paṛā iṃreji sei premer upakhyān.

Dukher tāpe jbale jbale abaśeṣe nibla māyer tāp;
Saṃsārete ekā paṛlen bāp.
Baṛo chele bās kare tār strīputrader sāthe
Bideśe patnāte.
Dui meye tār keu thāke nā kāche,
Śbaśurbāṛi āche.
Ekṭi thāke pharidpure,
Ārek meye thāke āro dūre
Madrāje kon bindhyagirir pār
Paṛla manjulikār 'pare bāper sebābhār.
Rāṁdhune brahmaner hāte khete karen ghriṇā,
Strīr rānnā binā
Annapāne hata nā tār ruci.
Sakālbelāy bhāter pālā, sandhyābelāy ruṭi kiṃbā luci;
Bhāter sange mācher ghatā
Bhājābhuji hata pāṁcṭāchaṭā;
Pāṃṭhā hata ruṭilucir sāthe.
Manjulikā dubelā sab āgāgoṛā rāṁdhe āpan hāte.
Ekādaśī ityādi tār sakal tithitei
Rāṁdhār pharda ei.
Bāper ghaṛti āpni moche jhāṛe
Roudre diye garam poṣāk āpni tole pāṛe.
Deske bākse kāgajpatra sājāy thāke thāke,
Dhobār bāṛir pharda tuke rākhe.
Gaylānī ār mudir hisāb rākhte ceṣṭā kare,
Ṭhik dite bhul hale takhan bāper kāche dhamak kheye

what could be more unrighteous than that in the three worlds.
In the dry pages of your scriptures no heart is to be found.
In the heart of all knowing God compassion does abound."

The father smiled a little. "Women," he thought,
"are balloons filled with hot air of heartbreak.
That life is a trying journey they are unaware."
Thinking so, he resumed reading the English romance.

Smouldering in sorrow the mother's suffering ended at last.
The father became lonely in this world.
The elder son lived in another part, in Patna,
with his wife and children.
The other two daughters were not at hand.
They had the households of their husbands.
One lived in Faridpur, the other daughter
lived far away, in Madras, beyond the *Bindhyas*.
On Manjulika's shoulder fell the burden of father's care.
He hated food cooked by hired help.
He didn't enjoy food in his life
unless it was cooked by his wife
Feasting with rice in the morning, roti or *luchi* in the evening;
along with five or six side-dishes,
with rice would be delicacies of fish,
and mutton curry with luchi was the normal fare.
Twice a day Manjulika cooked them all with care.
And on the *day of austerity* too,
the same menu everyday was his due.
She herself cleaned and dusted her father's bedroom
as she sun-dried his woollen garments before storing them.
Neatly she arranged the papers on his desk
and to track the laundry items she tried her best.
To keep the accounts of the grocer and the milkmaid
she gave all the care. Slightest error earned her father's censure.

mare.

Kāsundi tār konomatei hay nā māyer mato,
Tāi niye tār kata
Nāliś śunte hay.
Tā chāṛā tār pāñsājāṭā maner mato nay.
Māyer saṅge tulanāte padepadei ghaṭe ȳe tār truṭi.
Moṭāmuṭi—
Ājkālkār meyerā keu nay sekāler mato.
Haye nīrab nata,
Manjulī sab sahya kare, sarbadāi se śānta,
Kāj kare aklānta.
Ȳeman kare mātā bāraṃbār
Śiśu cheler sahasra ābdār
Hese sakal bahan karen sneher koutuke,
Temni karei suprasanna mukhe
Manjuli tār bāper nāliś danḍe danḍe śone,
Hāse mane mane.
Bābār kāche māyer smriti katai mūlyabān
Sei kathāṭā mane kare garbasukhe pūrṇa tāhār prāṇ.
"Āmār māyer ȳatna ȳējan peyeche ekbār
Ār kichu ki pachanda hay tār."

Holir samay bāpke sebār bāte dharla bhāri.
Pāṛāy pulin karchila daktāri,
Dakte hala tāre.
Hridȳantra bikal hate pāre
Chila eman bhay.
Pulinke tāi diner madhye bārebārei āste ȳete hay.
Mañjulī tār sane
Sahajbhābe kaibe kathā ȳatai bhābe mane
Tatai bādhe āro.
Eman bipad kāro
Hay ki konodin.
Galāṭi tār kāṁpe kena, kena etai kṣīṇ.
Cokher pātā kena

She could never make the mustard sauce like her mother.
Complaints about it
were a normal affair.
Besides, her *paan-treat* was not to his taste.
Couldn't come close to her mother though she did her best.
The bottom line was that
girls these days were not the same as before.
Keeping her head low
in silence Manjuli suffered all blows. She was ever calm
and toiled all day long.
As a mother with smile and in jest
tends to a child's thousands of requests.
Time and again Manjuli also
listened to all her father's complaints,
laughing in her sleeves.
Her heart was filled with the happiness of pride
to see how precious to her father was the memory of her mother.
"Can anything else satisfy the one who had the pleasure
of my mother's care!"

During the spring festival the father had a severe bout of gout.
Pulin was practising medicine nearby.
So he had to be called.
The heart could fail;
that was the scare.
So many times a day Pulin had to come.
The more Manjuli
tried to talk to him at ease
the more she was at unease.
Does such tragedy
strike anybody?
Why did her voice shake, why was it so faint,
why did her eyelids

Kiser bhāre jaṛiye āse ȳena.
Bhaye mare birahiṇī
Śunte ȳena pābe keha rakte ȳe tār bāje rinirini.
Padmapātāy śiśir ȳena, mankhāni tār buke
Dibārātri ṭalche kena emantaro dharāpaṛār mukhe.

Byāmo sere āse krame,
Gāmṭer byāthā anek ela kame.
Rogī śaȳya cheṛe
Ekṭu ekhan cale hāṁṭpā neṛe.
Eman samay sandhyābelā
Hāoyāy ȳakhan ȳuthībaner parānkhāni melā,
Āṁdhār ȳakhan cāṁder sange kathā balte ȳeye
Cup kare śeṣ tākiye thāke ceye
Takhan pulin rogīsebār parāmarśāchale
Manjulīre pāśer ghare deke bale—
"Jāna tumi tomār māyer sadh chila ei cite
Moder doṁhār biye dite.
Se icchāṭi tāṃri
Purāte cāi ȳeman karei pāri.
Eman kare ār kena din kaṭāi michimichi."

"Nā nā, chi chi, chi chi."
Ei bale se manjulikā dūhat diye mukhkhāni tār dheke
Chute gela gharer theke.
Āpan gharer duār diye paṛla mejher 'pare—
Jharjhariye jharjhariye buk phete tār aśru jhare paṛe.
Bhāble, "poṛā maner kathā eṛāyni oṃr cokh.
Ār kena go. Ebār maraṇ hok."

Manjulikā bāper sebāy lāgla dbigun kare
Āṣṭa prahar dhare.
Ābaśyakṭā sārā hale takhan lāge anābaśyak kāje,

become heavy with something indeed?
The forlorn girl was scared to death,
lest someone could hear the tinkling of her blood.
Like the dewdrops on a lotus leaf her
heart trembled within for the fear of exposure.

Gradually abated the sickness and
the pain in joints became much less.
Leaving his bed the patient
was moving around a bit.
At this time in the evening when
the wind unfurled the heart of the jasmine boughs,
the darkness, wishing to talk to the moon,
could only gaze in silence, at that time
on the pretext of discussing the patient's case
Pulin, taking Manjuli to the next room, said,
"You know that your mother had the desire
to unite us in marriage.
I want to satisfy her desire
in any way I can.
Why should we waste time any more?"

"No, no, shame, shame, shame."
So saying Manjulika ran out of the room,
covering her face with both hands.
Shutting her door she sprawled on the floor.
Tears rained, breaking her heart.
She thought, "His eyes can read my mind!
nothing anymore, let death be mine."

Round the clock, twice as hard as ever,
Manjulika became busy with father's care.
She did non-essentials after doing the basic chores
and washed the dishes that were washed before.
After a few hours

Ȳēbāsanṭā mājā hala ābār seṭā māje.
Dūtin ghāntā par
Ekbār ȳēghar jheṛeche pher jhāṛe sei ghar.
Kakhan ȳe snān, kakhan ȳe tār āhār,
Thik chila nā tāhār.
Kājer kāmāi chila nā ko ȳatakṣan nā rātri egāroṭāy
Śrānta haye āpni ghume mejher 'pare loṭāy.
Ȳe dekhla sēi abāk haye raila ceye,
Balle, "dhanyi meye."

Bāp śune kay buk phuliye, "garba kari nāko,
Kintu tabu āmār meye seṭā smaraṇ rekho.
Brahmacarȳa brata
Āmār kāchei śikṣā ȳe or. Naile dekhte anya rakam hata.
Ājkālkār dine
Saṃȳameri kaṭhor sādhan bine
Samājete ray nā kono bam̐dh,
Meyerā tāi śikhche kebal bibiyānār chām̐d."

Strīr maraner pare ȳabe
Sabemātra egāro mās habe,
Gujab gela śonā
Ei bāṛite ghatak kare ānāgonā.
Pratham śune manjulikār hay niko biśbās,
Tār pare sab rakam dekhe chāṛle se niśbās.
Byasta sabāi, kemantaro bhāb
Āsche ghare nānā rakam biliti āsbāb.
Dekhle bāper natun kare sājsajjā śuru,
Haṭhat kālo bhramarkriṣna bhuru,
Pākācul sab kakhan hala kaṭā,
Cādarete ȳakhantakhan gandha mākhār ghatā.

Mār kathā āj manjulikār paṛla mane
Bukbhanā ek biṣam byathār sane.
Hok nā mrityu, tabu
Ebāṛir ei hāoyār saṅge biraha tār ghaṭe nāi to kabhu.

again she swept the same room.
There was no fixed time for her bath
nor for her meals.
Until eleven at night her work never stopped
when in exhaustion on the floor she dropped.
Whoever noticed gave an amazed look.
"Marvellous girl!" they said.

Hearing that the father said, puffing his chest, "Bragging is not for me.
But you must remember that my daughter is she.
The teaching on chastity
she learnt from me. Otherwise how different it would be.
In these days
social structure can't be preserved
without strict self-control,
that's why women are western style prone."

When *eleven·months* were to pass
after the wife's death
the rumour spread about
frequent visits by the matchmaker to the house.
Manjulika could not believe it at first
but after checking she let out a deep sigh at last.
Everybody was busy, strange began to happen—
much imported furniture came into the house,
she saw her father's new grooming style,
dark as the bees became his eyebrows,
grey hair turned brownish
and perfume he splashed on his wrapper whenever he pleased.

Along with a heart wrenching pain
Manjulika now remembered her mother again.
She might be dead
but from this house she had never parted.
Her sweet and gracious image was

Kalyāṇi sei mūrtikhāni sudhāmākhā
E saṃsārer marme chila āṁkā;
Sādhbir sei sādhanpuṇya chila gharer mājhe,
Tāri paraś chila sakal kāje.
E saṃsāre tāṁr habe āj param mrityu, biṣam apamān
Sei bhebe ye manjulikār bhene paṛla prāṇ.
Cheṛe lajjābhay
Kanyā takhan niḥsaṃkoce kay
Bāper kāche giye,—
"Tumi naki karte yābe biye.
Āmrā tomār chelemeye natnināti yata
Sabār māthā karbe nata?
Māyer kathā bhulbe tabe?
Tomār prān ki eta kaṭhin habe."

Bābā balle śuṣka hese,
"Kaṭhin āmi kei bā jāne nā se?
Āmār pakṣe biye karā biṣam kaṭhor karma,
Kintu grihadharma
Stri nā hale apūrṇa ye ray
Manu hate mahābhārat sakal śastre kay.
Sahaj to nay dharmapathe hāṁṭā,
E to kebal hriday niye nayko kaṁdākaṭā.
Ye kare bhay duḥkha nite duḥkha dite
Se kāpuruṣ kenai āse prithibite."

Bākharganje meyer bāper ghar.
Sethāy gelen bar.
Biyer kadin āge. Bouke niye śeṣe
Yakhan phire elen deśe,
Gharete nei manjulikā. Khabar pelen ciṭhi paṛe
Pulin tāke biye kare
Geche doṁhe pharākkābād cale,
Seikhānetei ghar pātbe bale.
Āgun haye bāp
Bāre bāre dilen abhiśāp.

✿✿✿✿✿

etched in the heart of this household.
The merits of that devoted wife was, as it were,
in the family and her touch was everywhere.
It will now be her ultimate death, supreme insult—
this very thought broke Manjulika's heart.
Abandoning shame and fear
the daughter, in no uncertain way,
told her father —
"Is it true that you are marrying again
and bringing shame to us —
all your children and grandchildren?
Will you erase mother's memory?
Could your heart be so stony?"

The father said with a dry smile,
"Who doesn't know that I'm stone-hearted?
It is very difficult for me to marry once more.
But a householder's duty *remains incomplete*
without a wife.
From Manu¡ to the *Mahabharata* — all scripture say the same.
The path of righteousness isn't easy to tread
it is not merely crying over soft sentiment.
"I don't know why the cowards, afraid of accepting
or inflicting sorrow come into the world at all?"

The bride was from Bakarganj,
so a few days before wedding
the groom went there. When he returned
home with his wife at last
Manjulika was not there. He learnt from a letter —
Pulin had left with her
for Farakkabad after their marriage
to settle there.
In his rage
the father cursed them time and again.

✿✿✿✿✿

Mahuā (1929)

Sabalā

Nārīre āpan bhāgya jay karibār
Kena nāhi dibe adhikār
He bidhātā?
Nata kari māthā
Pathaprānte kena raba jāgi
Klāntadhairȳa pratyāśār pūraṇer lāgi
Daibāgata dine.

Sudhu śunye ceye raba? Kena nije nāhi laba cine
Sarthaker path.
Kena nā chutāba teje sandhāner rath
Durdharṣa aśbere bāṁdhi driḍha balgāpāśe.
Durjay āśbāse
Durgamer durga hate sādhanār dhan
Kena nāhi kari āharaṇ
Prān kari paṇ.

Ȳaba nā bāsarkakṣe badhubeśe bājāye kiṅkiṇī,
Āmāre premer bīrȳe kara aśaṅkini.
Bīrhaste baramālya laba ekdin
Se lagna ki ekānte bilīn
Kṣīṇadipta godhulite.
Kabhu tāre diba nā bhulite
Mor dripta kaṭhinatā.
Binamra dīnatā
Sammāner ȳogya nahe tār,
Phele debo ācchādan durbal lajjār.
Dekhā habe kṣubdha sindhutīre;
Taraṅgagarjanocchbās milaner bijaydhbānire
Diganter bakṣe nikṣepibe.

Indian Butter Tree (1929)

The Strong

Oh God,
why wouldn't You give woman
the right to control her own destiny?
With head bowed down
why should I remain awake on the wayside
with exhausted patience for the fulfilment of my hopes
some day to come by chance?

Should I only stare at the emptiness? Why should not I find
the path to fulfilment?
Why should not I drive fast the chariot of my quest
with the reins of the mighty horses firmly tied?
With indomitable expectation,
even at the cost of my life,
why should I not win
the treasure of my quest from its impenetrable fortress?

I shall not go into the bridal chamber as a bride with tinkling anklets.
Make me fearless with my love's prowess.
The day I may accept the garland of highest honour
with the hands of a victorious—is that moment
vanished in the faint light of the twilight?
My blazing determination
will never let it forget that.
The poverty of submissiveness
is not worthy of his respect.
The cover of weak shyness I shall abandon.

I shall meet on the angry ocean shore;
the thunderous waves will fling the victory shouts
to the horizon's heart.

Māthār gunṭhan khuli kaba tāre, martye bā tridibe
Ekmātra tumii āmār.
Samudrāpakhir pakṣe sei kṣaṇe uṭhibe huṃkār
Paścim paban hāni
Saptarṣīāloke ȳabe yābe tārā panthā anumāni.

He bidhātā, āmāre rekhonā bākyahīnā,
Rakte mor jāge rudrabīṇā.
Uttariyā jībaner sarbonnata muhūrter 'pare
Jībaner sarbottam bāṇī ȳena jhare
Kaṇṭha hate
Nirbārita srote.
Ȳāhā mor anirbacanīya
Tāre ȳena citta mājhe pāy mor priya.
Samay phurāy ȳadi, tabe tār pare
Śānta hok sēnirjhar naiḥśabdyer nistabdha sāgare.

Removing the sari from my head I'll tell him,
you are only mine on this earth or in the three worlds.
At that moment a roar will rise in the wings of the marine birds.
Forcing through the west wind
they will fly on their intuition towards the light
of the constellation of the *seven sages.*

Oh God, do not keep me mute, for
in my blood plays the trumpet of the furious.
Arriving at the highest moment of my life,
may my life's supreme message
pour like a waterfall into
the unrestrained stream.
May my beloved find in my heart
what is ineffable in me.
Then if my time comes to an end may that waterfall
attain serenity in the motionless ocean of silence.

Punaśca (1932)

Chemṛā kagajer jhuṛi

Bābā ese śudhālen,
'Ki karchis suni.
Kāpar kena tulis bakse, yābi kothāy?'

Sunritār ghar tintalāy.
Dakṣin dike dui jānālā,
Sāmne pālanka,
Bichānā lakhnoūchiṭe dhākā.
Anya deyāle lekhbār ṭebil,
Tār koṇe māyer phoṭograph,
Tini gechen mārā.
Bābār chabi deyāle,
Phreme jaṛāno mālā.
Mejete lāl śataraṅce
Śāri, śemij, blāuj,
Mojā rumāl chaṛāchaṛi.
Kukurṭā kāṁch gheṣe lej nāṛche,
Ṭhelā dicche kole thābā tule
Bhebe pācche nā kiser āyojan,
Bhay hacche pāche oke phele rekhe ābār yāy kothāo.
Choṭo bon samitā base āche hāṁṭu uṁcu kare,
Bāirer dike mukh phiriye.
Cul bāṁdhā hay ni,
Cokh duṭi rāṅā kānnār abasāne.
Cup kare raila sunritā,
Mukh nicu kare se kāpaṛ gochāy—
Hāt kāṁpe.
Bābā ābār ballen,
Suni kothāo yābi nāki.'
Sunritā śakta kare balle, 'tumi to baleicho,

Postscript (1932)

Basket of Shredded Papers

The father came to ask,
"What are you doing, Suni?
Why are you packing your suitcase, where are you going?"

Sunrita's room was on the third floor.
Two windows on the south
facing the bed,
covered with a bed-cover of Lucknow-motif.
By the other wall was her writing table
with her mother's photograph in one corner.
She had passed away.
Her father's picture was on the wall,
a flower garland draping the frame.
Scattered on the red throw rug on the floor were
her sari, chemise, blouse,
socks and handkerchiefs.
The dog, waging his tail, was brushing against her,
nudging her with his paws.
Unable to figure out what for the arrangements were
the dog was afraid that she would go somewhere leaving him behind.
The younger sister, Shamita, was squatting on the floor with
her legs folded upwards and her face turned towards outside.
Her tresses were unbraided,
eyes red from crying.
Sunrita, maintaining her silence,
was gathering her clothes,
her hands shaking.
The father asked again,
"Suni, are you going somewhere?"
Sunrita said firmly, "You have told already that

E bāṛite hate pāre nā āmār biye,
Āmi ȳāba anuder bāsāy.'
Śamitā balle, 'chi chi, didi, kī balcha.'
Bābā ballen, ' orā ȳe mānenā āmāder mat.'
'Tabu oder mati ȳe āmāke mānte habe ciradin,'
Ei bale suni sephtipin bhare rākhle lephāphāy.
Driḍha or kaṇṭhasbar, kaṭhin or mukher bhāb,
Saṃkalpa abicalita.
Bābā ballen, 'aniler bāp jāt māne,
Se ki rāji habe.'
Sagarbe bale uṭhla sunritā,
'Cena nā tumi anilbābuke,
Tāṁr joṛ āche pouruṣer, tāṁr mat tāṁr nijer.'
Dirghanisbās phele bābā cale gelen ghar theke,
Śamitā uṭhe tāṁke jaṛiye dharle,
Beriye gela tār sange.
Bājla dupurer ghanṭā.
Sakāl theke khāoyā nei sunritār.
Śamitā ekbār esechila dākte,
O balle, khābe bandhur bāṛi giye.
Mā-marā meye, bāper ādure,
Minati karte āschilen tini;
Śamitā path āgliye balle,
'Kakkhano ȳete pārbe nā bābā,
O nā khāy to nei khela.'

Jānlā theke mukh bāṛiye
Dekhle sunritā rāstār dike,
Eseche anuder gāṛi.
Tārātāri culṭā āṁcṛiye
Brocṭā lāgācche ȳakhan kāṁdhe,
Śami ese balle, 'Ei nāo tāder ciṭhi.'
Bale phele dila chuṁṛe or kole.
Śunritā paṛla ciṭhikhānā,

the marriage can't take place in this house.
I'll go to Anu's house."
Shamita said, "Shame on you, *Didi*, what are you saying?"
The father said, "But they don't agree with our opinion."
"Yet I'll have to abide by their opinion all my life."
So saying Suuni packed the safety pins in an envelope.
Firm was her voice, stony was her face,
unshakable was her resolve.
The father said, "Anil's father believes in the caste system.
Will he agree to this?"
Proudly declared Sunrita,
"You don't know Anilbabu at all;
he has strength in his manliness. He follows his conviction."
The father left the room with a deep sigh.
Shamita got up and left,
her arms twining around her father.

The clock struck noon.
Sunrita had taken nothing since the morning.
Shamita had once come to call her,
but she said that she would eat in her friend's house.
Motherless girl, father's pet,
he was coming to cajole her.
Shamita stood in his way.
"You can never go, father,
she doesn't have to eat if she doesn't want to."

Sunrita looked at the street
poking her head through the window.
Anu's car was standing there.
After combing her hair in a hurry when
she was about to pin the brooch on her shoulder
Shami came and said, "Here is a letter from them."
So saying, she threw it on her lap.
Sunrita read the letter,

Mukh haye gela phyākāśe,
Base paṛla toranger upar.
Ciṭhite āche
'Bābār mat karte pārba niścita chila mane,
Hala nā kichutei,—
Kajei—.'

Bājla ekṭā.
Śuni cup kare base, cokhe jal nei.
Rāmcarit balle ese,
'Motor dāṃṛiye anek kṣaṇ.'
Suni balle, 'ȳte bale de.'
Kukurṭā kāche ese base raila cup kare.
Bābā bujhlen,
Praśna karlen nā,
Ballen or māthāy hāt buliye,
'Cal suni, hosengābāde, tor māmār okhāne.'

Kāl biyer din.
Anil jid karechila habe nā biye.
Mā byathita haye balechila, 'thāknānā.'
Bāp balle, 'pagal nāki.'
Elektrik batir mālā khātano hacche bāṛite,
Samasta din bājche sānāi.
Huhu kare uṭhche aniler manṭā.'

Takhan sandhyā sāṭṭā.
Sunider boubājārer bāṛir ektalāy
Ḍābāhuṃko bāṃ hāte dhare tāmāk khācche
Kailes sarkār,
Ār tālpātār pākhāy bātās calche ḍān hāte;
Behārāke dekeche pā ṭipe debe.
Kālimākhā maylā jājime kāgajpatra rāś karā;
Jbalche ekṭā kerosin lanthan.
Hathāt anil ese upasthit.

her face turned paper-white,
she sat down on the suitcase.
The letter said —
"I was sure that I would be able to get father's consent
but I could not by any means.
So .... "

The clock struck one.
Suni was sitting in silence, no tears in her eyes.
Ramcharit came to say,
"The car has been waiting for a long time."
Suni said, "Tell him to leave."
The dog came and sat beside her.
The father understood,
he asked no question.
Caressing her head he said,
"Shuni, let us go to Hosengabad, to your maternal uncle."

The wedding was on the following day.
Anil had insisted that there would be no wedding.
His aggrieved mother had said, "Let it be so."
His father said, "Are you out of your mind!"
The house was being decorated with strings of electric lights,
the *shahnai* had been playing all day long.
Anil's heart was aching.

It was seven o'clock in the evening.
Kailas Sarkar, sitting in the ground floor of Suni's house
in Bowbazar, was smoking tobacco from
the coconut-shell hookah in his left
and fanning with a palm-leaf-fan in his right hand.
He had just called for his servant to massage his feet.
Papers were piled high on the mattress blackened with grime.
A kerosene lantern was burning.
All of a sudden Anil appeared there.

Kailes śaśabyasta uṭhe dāṃṛālo
Śithil kāchākoṁchā sāmliye.
Anil balle,
'Pārbaṇīṭā bhulechilem golmāle,
Tāi esechi dite.'
Tār pare bādhōbādho galāy balle,
'Amni dekhe ȳaba tomāder sunididir gharṭā.'

Gela ghare.
Khāṭer upaṛ base raila māthāy hāt diye.
Kiser ektā aspaṣṭa gandha,
Murchiter niśbāser mato.
Se gandha culer nā śukno phuler,
Nā śūnya ghare sañcita bijaṛita smritir,
Bichānay, coukite, pardāy.
Sigāret dhariye ṭānla kichukṣaṇ,
Chuṁṛe phele dila jānālār bāire.
Ṭebiler nīce theke cheṁṛā kāgajer jhuṛiṭā
Nila kole tule.
Dhak kare uṭhla buker madhye;
Dekhle, jhuṛībharā rāśi rāśi cheṁṛā cithi,
Phike nīl raṅer kāgaje
Anileri hāte lekhā.
Tār sange ṭukro ṭukro cheṁṛā ektā phoṭograph.
Ār chila bachar cār āgekār
Duṭi phul, lāl phitey bāṁdhā
Medeñheyār pātār sange
Śukno pyānsi ār bhāyolet.

❁❁❁❁❁

Kailas stood up in a huff,
pulling together his slackened garb.
Anil said,
"As I was busy I forgot about your tips;
so I've come to pay it."
In a hesitant voice he said then,
"Since I am here I might as well see the room of your Sunididi."

He went into the room.
He sat on the bedstead, his hand resting on his head.
There was an obscure smell of something,
like the breath of an unconscious person.
The smell was not of hair or dry flowers,
nor was it of the accumulated memories
enmeshed in the bed, bedstead and the drapes.
He lighted a cigarette and smoked for a while
and tossed it out through the window.
He took the waste paper basket on his lap
from under the table.
Anil felt a jolt in his heart;
he saw a basket full of ripped letters,
written on light blue papers
in his own hand.
Along with those was a shredded photograph.
Also there were two flowers tied to
a maidenhair leaf with a red ribbon—
a dry pansy and a violet
from four years back.

Punaśca

Sādhāraṇ meye

Āmi antaḥpurer meye,
Cinbe nā āmāke.
Tomār śeṣ galper baiṭi paṛechi, śarattbābu,
'Bāsi phuler mālā.'
Tomār nāyikā elokeśir maraṇdaśā dharechila
Paymtriś bachar bayase,
Paṁciś bachar bayaser sange chila tār reṣāreṣi,
Dekhlem tumi mahadāśay baṭe,
Jitiye dile tāke.

Nijer kathā bali.
Bayas āmār alpa.
Ekjaner man chumyechila
Āmar ei kāṁcā bayaser māyā.
Tāi jene pulak lāgta āmār dehe—
Bhule giyechilem, atyanta sādhāraṇ meye āmi.
Āmār mato eman āche hājār hājār meye,
Alpabayaser mantra tāder ȳoubane.

Tomāke dohāi dii,
Ekṭi sādhāraṇ meyer galpa lekho tumi.
Baṛo duḥkha tār.
Tāro sbabhāber gabhire
Asādhāraṇ ȳadi kichu taliye thāke kothāo,
Keman kare pramāṇ karbe se,
Eman ka jan mele ȳarā tā dharte pāre.
Kāṁcā bayaser jādu lāge oder cokhe,
Man ȳay nā satyer khoṁje,
Āmrā bikiye ȳai maricikār dāme.
Kathāṭā kena uṭhla tā bali.

Postscript (1932)

Ordinary Woman

I am a woman, stuck indoors.
You wouldn't know me.
I've read your latest novel, *Saratbabu*.
'It's a garland of withered flowers.'
Your heroine Elokeshi was in a trance
at the age of thirty-five.
She had some sort of competition with twenty-five year olds,
no, you are generous indeed;
you made her the winner.

Let me speak about myself.
I am young in age.
The fancy of my green years
touched someone's heart.
My body used to shiver at that thought—
I forgot I was a very ordinary woman.
There are millions of women like me
with the enchantment of their youth.

I beseech you!
Please write a story about an ordinary woman.
She is very unhappy.
If there is something uncommon buried
in the depth of her nature,
how can she prove or
even how many are there who can recognise it?
The fancy of tender age is in their eyes.
Not seeking the real
we sell ourselves for the price of a mirage.
Let me tell why I am saying this.

Mane karo tār nām nareś.
Se balechila keu tār cokhe paṛe ni āmār mato.
Etabaṛo kathāṭā bisbās karba ȳe sāhas hay nā,
Nā karba ȳe eman jor koi.

Ekdin se gela bilete.
Ciṭhipatra pāi kakhono bā.
Mane mane bhābi, rām rām̃ Eta meyeo āche se deśe,
Eta ṭhelaṭheli bhīṛ Ār tārā ki sabāi asāmānya,
Eta buddhi, eta ujjbalatā.
Ār tārā sabāi ki ābiṣkār kareche ek nareś senke
Sbadeśe ȳar paricay cāpā chila daśer madhye.

Gela meler ciṭhite likheche
Lijir sange giyechila samudre nāite.
Baṅāli kabir kabitā kālāin diyeche tule,
Sei ȳekhāne urbaśī uṭheche samudra theke.
Tār pare bālir 'pare basla pāśāpāśi—
Sāmne dulche nīl samudrer dheu
Ākāśe chaṛāno nirmal sūrȳalok.
Liji tāke khub āste āste balle,
'Ei se din tumi esecha, dudin pare ȳābe cale;
Jhinuker duṭi kholā,
Mājhkhānṭuku bharā thāk
Ekṭi niret aśrubindu diye—
Durlabh, mūlyahīn.'
Kathā balbār ki asāmānya bhangi.
Sei sange nareś likheche,
'Kathāguli yādi bānāno hay doṣ kī,
Kintu camatkār—
Hīrēbasāno sonār phul ki satya, tabuo ki satya nay.'
Bujhtei pārcha,
Ekṭā tulonār saṁket or ciṭhite adriśya kaṁṭār mato
Āmār buker kāche biṁdhiye diye jānāy—
Āmi atyanta sādhāraṇ meye.

Let us assume that his name is Naresh.
He said that he hadn't seen anyone like me.
I don't have the courage to believe such a grand statement
nor do I have the strength not to.

He went to England at some point in time.
Sometimes I get his letters.
I say to myself, for goodness sakes, so many women are there!
A crowd of them, pushing and shoving!
And how extraordinary they are,
so intelligent and so bright!
Have all of them discovered one Naresh Sen
whose particulars were buried among many in his country?

In his last mail he wrote that
he had gone with Lizzie for a swim in the ocean.
He quoted a few lines from a poem of a *Bengali poet*
where Urbashi, the heavenly nymph, rises from the ocean.
Then they sat, side by side, on the sand;
before them was the rocking of the waves of the blue sea,
the sky was flooded with bright sunshine.
Lizzie whispered into his ears,
"You came only the other day and you'll go away in a while;
two shells of an oyster
let the inside be filled with a solid drop of tear—
rare, priceless."
What an extraordinary way of speaking!
Along with that Naresh wrote,
"It is not wrong even if the words be made up,
but beautiful —
A golden flower studded with diamonds is not real, yet isn't it so."
Surely you can understand,
the hint of a simile in the letter jabbed me
close to my heart declaring —
I am a very ordinary woman.

Mūlyabānke puro mūlya cukiye dii
Eman dhan nei āmār hāte.
Ogo, nāhay tāi hala,
Nā hay rhiṇīi railem cirajīban.
Pāye paṛi tomār, ekṭā galpa lekha tumi, śaratbābu,
Nitāntai sadhāraṇ meyer galpa—
Ȳe durbhaginike dūrer theke pāllā dite hay
Antata pāṁcsātjan asāmānyār sange—
Arthāt, saptarathinīr mār.
Bujhe niyechi āmār kapāl bheṅeche,
Hār hayeche āmār.
Kintu tumi ȳar kathā likhbe,
Tāke jitiye diyo āmār haye,
Paṛte paṛte buk ȳena oṭhe phule
Phulcandan paṛuk tomār kalamer mukhe.
Tāke nām diyo mālatī.
Oi nāmṭā āmār.
Dharā paṛbār bhay nei;
Eman anek mālaṭī āche baṅlādeśe,
Tārā sabāi samānya meye.
Tārā phārasi jārmān jāne na,
Kāṁdte jāne.

Kī kare jitiye debe.
Ucca tomār man, tomār lekhanī mahiyasī.
Tumi hayto oke niye ȳābe tyāger pathe,
Duḥkher carame, śakuntalār mato.
Dayā koro āmāke.
Neme eso āmār samatale.
Bichānāy śuye śuye rātrir andhakāre
Debatār kāche ȳe asambhab bar māgi—
Se bar āmi pābo nā,
Kintu pāy ȳena tomār nāyikā.
Rākhōnā kena nareśke sāt bachar landane,
Bāre bāre phel karuk tār parikṣāy,

I have no treasure to pay in full
the value of the invaluable.
Well, let it be so.
Let me be indebted all my life.
I humbly entreat you. Please write a story, Saratbabu,
about an utterly ordinary woman—
The unfortunate one who has to compete from a distance
with at least five or seven extraordinary women —
in other words competing with *seven goddesses.*
I know that my luck has ran out
and I have been beaten.
But make the woman about whom you are going to write
victorious on my behalf.
Let my chest puff up while reading
and may all the glory come to your pen.
You may name her Malati.
That is my name.
But there is no chance of finding her identity.
There are so many Malatis like this in Bengal
and they are all ordinary women.
They don't know the French or the German.
They know only to feel sorry for themselves.

How you'll make her victorious.
Generous is your heart, all powerful is your pen.
You will probably be inclined to lead her into the path
of sacrifice,
into extreme sorrow, like *Shakuntala.*
Please have pity on me.
Come down to my level.
Lying in my bed in the darkness of night,
the unattainable boon that I seek from the gods
I'll not get that boon.
But let your heroine get it.
Why don't you keep Naresh in London for seven years,
let him flunk his exams again and again,

Ādare thāk āpan upāsakmandalīte.
Itimadhye mālati paś karuk em. e.
Kalkātā biśbabidyālaye,
Gaṇite hok pratham tomār kalamer ek āṁcaṛe.
Kintu oikhāne ȳadi thāma
Tomār sāhityasamrāṭ nāme paṛbe kalaṅka.
Āmār daśā ȳai hok
Khāṭo koro nā tomār kalpanā.

Tumi to kripaṇ nao bidhātār mato.
Meyeṭāke dāo pāṭhiye yurope.
Sekhāne ȳarā jñānī, ȳarā bidbān, ȳārā bīr,
Ȳārā kabi, ȳarā śilpī, ȳarā rājā,
Dal beṁdhe āsuk or cār dike.
Jyotirbider mato ābiskār karuk oke,
Śudhu biduṣī bale nay, narī bale.
Or madhye ȳe biśbabijayī jādu āche
Dharā paṛuk tār rahasya, mūḍher deśe nay,
Ȳe deśe āche samajhdār, āche daradi,
Āche iṃrej jarmān phārāsi.
Mālatir sammāner janya sabhā ḍākā hoknā,
Baṛo baṛo nāmjādār sabhā.
Mane karā yāk sekhāne barṣaṇ hacche muṣaldhāre caṭubākya,
Mājhkhān diye se caleche abahelāy—
Dheuer upar diye ȳena pāler nouko.
Or cokh dekhe orā karche kānākāni,
Sabāi balche bhāratbarṣer sajal megh ār ujjbal roudra
Mileche or mohinī drisṭite.
(Eikhāne janāntike bale rākhi,
Srisṭikartār prasād satyai āche āmār cokhe.
Balte hala nijer mukhei,
Ekhano kono yuropīya rasajñer
Sākṣāt ghate ni kapāle.)!
Nareś ese dāṁṛāk sei koṇe,
Ār tār sei asāmānya meyer dal.

let his circle of admirers treat him tenderly.
Meanwhile let Malati get her M. A.,
from the Calcutta University.
Let her stand first in Mathematics with a stroke of your pen.
But if you stop there
your fame as the king of king-storytellers will be sullied.
Whatever may be my situation
don't stifle your imagination!

You are not close-fisted like God.
Send the poor woman to Europe.
All the learned, the scholars, the heroes there,
the poets, the artists and the monarchs —
let them crowd around her in droves.
Like astronomers let them discover her
not only as a scholar but also as a woman.
The world conquering magic that is in her,
let its mystery be evident, not in the *land of the ignorant*
but in the land of the connoisseurs, the appreciative
and where there are the English, the Germans and the French.
To honour Malati let meetings be arranged,
meetings of people with big name and fame.
Let us assume that flattering praises are being showered on her in buckets,
she is moving around unaffected
like a sailboat gliding over the waves.
Gazing at her eyes they are whispering among themselves.
Everyone is saying the water laden dark cloud and bright sunshine of India
have come together in her enchanting eyes.
(Let me say it aside,
the Creator's grace really fell on my eyes.
This had to come out from my own lips.
As my luck would have it
I haven't yet met any European connoisseur.)
Let Naresh stand in a corner
and his bevy of extraordinary admirers.

Ār tār pare?
Tār pare āmār naṭeśākṭi muṛola,
sbapna āmār phurola.
Hāy re samānya meye
Hāy re bidhātār śaktir apabyay.

And after that?
After that my paltry crop withered in drought.
An end came to my dream.
Alas ordinary woman!
Alas God's wasted power!

Prahāsinī (1935)

Ādhunikā

Ciṭhi taba paṛilām, balibār nāi mor,
Tāp kichu āche tāhe, santāp tāi mor.
Kabigiri phalābār utsāhābanyāy
Adhunikāder 'pare kariyāchi anyāy
Ȳadi sandeha kara eta baṛo abinay,
Cup kare ȳe sahibe se kakhano kabi nay.
Baliba dūcār kathā, bhālo mane śuno tā;
Pūraṇ kariyā niyo prakāśer nyūnatā.
Pāṁjite ȳe āṁk ṭāne grahānakṣattar
Āmi to tadanusāre periyechi sattar.
Āyur tabil mor kuṣṭhir hisābe
Ati alpa dineteyi śūnye miśābe.
Calite calite pathe ājkāl hardam
Buke lāge ȳamarathacakrer kardam.
Tabu mor nām ājo pāribe nā oṭhāte
Prātnik tattber gabeṣanākoṭhāte.
Jīrṇa jībane āj raṅ nāi, madhu nāi—
Mane rekho, tabu āmi janmechi adhunāi.
Sāṛe āṭhāro śatak e. d., se ȳe b. c. nay;
Mor ȳārā meyēbon nārader pisi nay.
Ādhunikā ȳāre bala tāre āmi cini ȳe,
Kabiȳaśe tāri kāche bāro ānā rhiṇī ȳe.
Tāri hāte ciradin ȳatparonāsti
Peyechi puraskār, peyechio śāsti.
Pramāṇ giyechi rekhe, e-kālinī ramaṇīr
Ramanīya tāle bāṁdhā chanda e dhamanir.
Kāche pāi hārāībā tabu tāri smritite
Surasourabh jāge ājo mor gītite.
Manoloke dūti ȳārā mādhurī nikunje
Gunjan kariyāchi tāhāderi gun ye.

Satire (1935)

Modern Woman

I read your letter and I have nothing to add.
I'm a bit dismayed, for disapprobation
was displayed. In the enthusiasm to display
my poetic caliber I have done injustice
to modern women. Whoever will silently
accept any hint of such vanity can never
be a poet. So I'll say a few things. Please listen
with open mind. You can round up the rough edges
of my expression. According to the indication
of the configuration of planets and stars
I have passed seventy. According to the
calculations of my horoscope the treasury
of my longevity will soon equal zero.
While walking these days the muck from the
god of death's chariot often sticks to my heart.
Yet you won't be able to relegate my name
to the archives of archaeology. This worn out
life now has no zing, has no honey. You must
keep in mind that I was yet born in modern times.
Eighteen and a half hundred A. D., it is not B. C.
Those who are my daughters or sisters are not
the aunts of the sage *Narad*. I know those who are
called modern women, as I am indebted to them
for at least three-quarters of my fame as a poet.
I got much reward from them and punishment
as well. I left proof of modern women, for
the rhythm of my heartbeat is tuned to them.
Whether I get them close or lose them yet
even to this day my songs come alive in their
glorious tune. I have always sung their glory, of
those who are (she) messengers in my world

Sekāleo kālidāsbararuciādirā
Purasundarider praśastabādirā
Ȳāder mahimāgāne jāgālen biṇāre
Tārāo sabāi chila adhunār kināre.
Ādhunikā chila nāko hena kāl chila nā,
Tāhāderi kalyāṇe kābyānuśilanā.
Puruṣ kabir bhāle āche kono sugraha,
Cirakāl tāi tāre eta mahānugraha.
Jutā-pāye, khāli-pāye slipāre bā nūpūre
Nabinārā ȳuge ȳuge ela dine dupure,
Ȳetha sbapaner pāṛā sethā ȳay āgiye,
Prāṇṭāke nāṛā diye gān ȳay jāgiye.
Tabu kabiracanāy ȳadi kono lalanā
Dekha akritajñata, jeno seṭā chalanā.
Miṭhe ār kaṭu mile, miche ār satyi,
Ṭhokāṭhuki kare hay rasutpatti.
Miṣṭa katur mājhe konṭā ȳe mithye
Se kathāṭā cāpā thāk kabir sāhitye.
Oi dekho, oṭā bujhi hala śleṣbākya.
Erakam bāṁkā kathā dhākā diye rākhya.
Pralobhanrūpe āse parihāspaṭutā,
Sāmlāno nāhi ȳay akāraṇ kaṭutā.
Bāre bāre ei mato kari atyukti
Kṣamā kare koro sei aparādhmukti.

Ār ȳāi bali nāko e kathāṭā balibai,
Tomāder dbāre morā bhikṣār thali bai.
Anna bhariyā dāo sudhā tāhe lukiye,
Mūlya tāhāri āmi ȳai kichu cukiye.
Anek geyechi gān mugdha e prāṇ diye—
Tomrā to śunecha tā, antata kān diye.
Karuṇāy bale thāka, "āhā, manda bā ki"
Khuṁṭe ber karo nā to kono chandāphāṁki.
Ei ṭuku ȳā mileche tāi pāy kajanā,
Eta lok kareche to bhāratir bhajanā.
Er par bāṁśi ȳabe phele ȳāba dhūlite

of felicity. Even in the past pioneer adulators
of beautiful women like *Kalidasa-Bararuchi*
made their *veena* come alive with praises of the
women who were all avant-garde. There was never a
time when there were no modern women and poetry
was cultivated only for their benefit. The male poets
were born under lucky stars and that is why grace was
always showered on them. Wearing shoes, slippers,
anklets or bare feet the avant-garde women
have come through the ages every morning and evening.
They enter the land of dreams, raising waves in the heart
and awakening songs. In spite of that if any lady finds
ingratitude in a poet's work it must be taken as
an illusion. The charm of poetry comes from mixing
sweet and bitter, true and false and from collision of the
opposites. Which is false between sweet and bitter
let it remain undisclosed in the poet's work.
Look here, if you think it is sarcasm keep such
comments to yourself. Humour and wit come as
temptation and unnecessary bitterness is
hard to control. With your pardon absolve me for
committing the crime of repeated hyperbole.

Whatever I may say I must add this:
We come to your doors with our begging bowls.
You fill them with goodies with hidden nectar.
I am paying only a fraction of its price.
I sang many songs from my bewitched heart
and you heard them at least with your ears.
Out of compassion you said, "Well, it is not bad."
You didn't seek the trifling error in the meter.
So many are worshipping the goddess of music
but how many get in return what I got!
At last when I'll leave my flute in the dust,
then forget me if you can. On that day,

Takhan āmāre bhulo pāro ȳadi bhulite.
Sedin nūtan kabi dakṣiṇpabane
Madhu rhitu mukharibe tomāder stabane—
Takhan āmār kono kīṭekāṭā pātāte
Ektā lāino ȳadi pāre man mātāte
Tāhale haṭhat buk uṭhibe ȳe kāṁpiyā
Baitaraṇīte ȳabe ȳāba kheyā cāpiyā.
E kī gero. Kāj ki e kalpanābihāre,
Senṭimenṭāliṭi bale loke ihāre.
Mare tabu bāṁcibār ābdār khokāmi,
Saṃsāre er ceye nei ghor bokāmi.
Eṭā to ādhunikār sahibe nā kichutei;
Esṭimeśane tār paṛe ȳaba nicutei.
Ataeb, man, tor kalsi o daṛi ān,
Atale maris dub miđbhikṭoriyān.
Kono phal phalibe nā āṁkhijalsicane;
Śukno hāsiṭā tabe rekhe ȳāi pichane.
Gadagada sur kena bidāyer paṭhṭay,
Śeṣ belā keṭe ȳak ṭhāṭṭay ṭhāṭṭāy.

Tomāder mukhe thāk hāsyer roṣnāi—
Kichu sīriyās kathā bali tabu, doṣ nai.
Kakhano diyeche dekhā hena prabhāśālinī
Sudhu ēkālinī nay, ȳārā cirakalinī.
E kathāṭā bale ȳāba mor kanpheśanei
Tāder milane kono kṣaniker neśā nei.
J̄ibaner sandhyāy tāhāderi baraṇe
Śeṣ rabirekhā rabe sonāāṁkā smaraṇe.
Sursuradhunīdhāre ȳe amrita uthale
Mājhe mājhe kichu tār jhare pare bhutale,
E janame se kathār jānār sambhābanā
Kemane ghaṭibe ȳadi sākṣāt pāba nā.
Āmāder kata truṭi āsane o śayane,
Kṣamā chila ciradin tāhāder nayane.
Premdīp jbelechila puṇyer āloke,
Madhur kareche tārā ȳata kichu bhāloke.
Nānārūpe bhogsudhā ȳā kareche baraṣan

a new poet in the southern breeze will fill
the sweet spring season with your adoration.
Then, even if a single line from my moth-eaten
pages can delight you, my heart will quiver
when I will cross the river to the abode of
the dead in the ferry boat. What nonsense!
What's the use of this day dreaming! People
call it sentimentality. He wants to live
even after death, what a childish fancy!
Modern women can never stand for it.
He will go down in their estimation.
So, my heart, bring your stone and rope and
you mid-Victorian, sink to the bottom.
Nothing will be gained by shedding tears;
so I leave my trite smile behind. Why sing
the blues at the time of parting
and not go laughing and joking!

May there be the glow of smile on your faces!
No harm will come if I say a few words in seriousness.
Seldom had appeared such glorious women
who were not of their time but of all times. I'll
say this as my confession that I have not a
moment's hope of meeting them. In the twilight days
of my life I'll leave the last glow of this *Rabi*
for their adoration. Occasionally a little
of the splendour, overflowing from the songs
of the heavenly Ganga, falls on this earth.
I know not how the opportunity of its taste
will come to me if I can't ever meet them.
At all times we fell short in their estimation,
yet forgiveness was always in their eyes.
They lit the lamp of love in the light of virtue
and made enchanting all that was good.
They showered delights in many forms and blessed
many things with their gentle touch. Who can take

Tāre śuci karechila sukumār paraśan.
Dāmī ȳāhā miliyāche j̄ibaner e pāre
Maraṇer t̄ire tāre niye ȳete ke pāre.
Tabu mane āśā kari mrityur rāteo
Tāhāderi prem ȳena nite pāri pātheya.
Ār beśi kāj nei, keṭe geche tin kāl,
Ȳe kāle esechi āj se kālṭā sinikāl
Kichu āche ȳar lāgi sugabh̄ir niśbās
Jege oṭheī dhākā thāk tār prati biśbās.
Ekṭu sabur karo, āro kichu bale ȳai,
Kathār caram pāre tārpare cale ȳai.
Ȳe giyeche tār lāgi khuṁciyonā cetana,
Chāyāre atithi kare āsanṭā peto nā.
Batsare batsare śok karā r̄itiṭār
Mithyār dhākkay bhit bhāṅe smritiṭār.
Bhiṛ kare ghaṭākarā dharābāṁdhā bilāpe
Pāche kono aparādh ghaṭe prathākhilāpe,
Bhārate chila nā leś ei sab kheyāler—
Kabī'pare bhār chila nij memoriyāler.
"Bhuliba nā, bhuliba nā" ei bale citkār
Bidhi nā śonen kabhu, balo tāhe hit kār.
Ȳe bholā sahaj bholā nijer alakhye
Sēi bhālo hridayer sbāsther pakṣe.
Śuṣka utsa khuṁje marumāṭi khoṁṛāṭā,
Telh̄in d̄ip lāgi deślāi poṛāṭā,
Ȳe moṣ kothāo nei sei moṣ tāṛāno,
Kāje lāgibe nā ȳāhā sei kāj bāṛāno—
Śaktir bāje byay ere kay jeno he,
Utsāha dekhābār sadupāy e nahe.
Mane jeno j̄ibanṭā maraneri jajñaī
Sthāȳi ȳahā, ār ȳāhā thākār aȳogya,
Sakali āhuti rūpe paṛe tāri śikhāte,
Ṭiṁke nā ȳā kathā diye ke pāribe ṭiṁkāte.
Chāi haye giye tabu bāki ȳahā rahibe
Āpanār kathā se to āpanii kahibe.

✽✽✽✽✽

along with him in death the precious things he has gained
in life? Yet, I keep this hope that in the night of my death
I can take their love as the fare for my last ferry.
There is nothing more to be done, as I've used
most of my life-span and reached a phase called
cynical! If there is something that stirs a deep sigh —
let my faith in them remain unrevealed.
Have a little patience, let me say a little more;
after finishing I shall part. Don't nudge your
conscience for the departed. Making the shadow
your guest, do not retain a seat for him to rest. The blow
from the vain tradition of condolence every year
shakes the foundation of memory. In India
there was no hint of the quaint practice —
showy display of sorrow every year
following a fixed recipe without any flaw
in the ritual. The poet was responsible
for his memorial. To shouts like "We won't
forget you, never forget you" — God turns
deaf ear. What good can come of it let me hear.
The oblivion that comes on its own
unconsciously is good for the heart.
Digging the desert sand to find the dry source,
to light a match for a lamp without oil,
to try to drive out the buffalo that isn't there,
to increase the load of work that is useless —
know these to be a waste of energy and not
the way to show your keenness. Remember
that life is the burnt-offering to death —
All that is durable, all that is unfit for enduring
becomes oblation in its flame. Words can't make
the transient permanent. Whatever will remain
after turning to ashes will speak its own message.

✽✽✽✽✽

Śyāmalī, 1936

Bāṁśioālā

"Ogo bāṁśioālā,
Bājāo tomār bāṁśi,
Śuni āmār nutan nām"
—Ei bale tomāke pratham ciṭhi likhechi,
Mane āche to?
Āmi tomār bāṁlādeśer meye.
Sriṣṭikartā puro samay den ni
Āmāke mānuṣ kare gaṛte,—
Rekhechen ādhāādhi kare.
Antare bāhire mil hay ni
Sekāle ār ājker kāle,
Mil hay ni byathāy ār buddhite,
Mil hay ni śaktite ār icchāy.
Āmāke tule den ni e yuger pārāni noukoy,
Calā āṭak kare phele rekhechen
Kālasroter o pāre bāludāṅāy.
Sekhān theke dekhi
Prakhar āloy jhāpsā dūrer jagat,—
Binā kārane kāṅāl man adhīr haye oṭhe,
Dui hāt bāṛiye dei,
Nāgāl pāi ne kichui kono dike.
Belā to kāṭe nā,
Base thāki joār–jaler dike ceye—
Bhese yāy mukti–pārer kheyā,
Bhese yāy dhanapatir diṅā,
Bhese yāy calti belār ālochāyā.
Eman samay bāje tomār bāṁśi
Bharā jībaner sure.
Marā diner nāḍir madhey
Dabdabiye phire āse prāṇer beg.

She Who is Dark, 1936

The Flute Player

"Oh, Flute-player,
please play your flute.
Let me hear my new name."
Thus I wrote my first letter,
do you remember it?
I am a girl from your Bengal.
The Creator did not spend the time
needed to make me a complete person.
He left me half done.
So there is no harmony between my heart within and without,
and the age long past and the present.
There is no concord between my pain and intellect
and no balance between my will and desire.
He did not put me in a modern ferryboat.
He stopped my journey and left me stuck
in the sandbank on the other side of the flow of time.
From there I see
the distant world blurred in blinding light.
For no reason, my thirsty mind becomes restless.
I stretch out my two arms
but can't touch anything anywhere.
My time does not pass.
I sit gazing at the water in high tide where
floats away the ferryboat to the land of free.
Floats away the wealthy merchant's boat and
floats away the light and shadow of the present.
At such a time your flute plays
the tune of a fulfilled life.
In my dead life's veins
life force surges back throbbing.

Ki bājāo tumi,
Jāni ne se sur jāgāy kār mane kī byathā.
Bujhi bājāo pañcamrāge
Dakṣiṇ hāoār nabayoubaner bhāṭiāri.
Śunte śunte nijeke mane hay—
Ye chila pahaṛtalir jhirjhire nadī,
Tār buke haṭhat uṭheche ghaniye
Śrābaner badalrātri.
Sakāle uṭhe dekhā yāy pāṛi geche bhese,
Ekgum̐ye pātharguloke ṭhelā dicche
Asahya sroter ghurṇi–mātan.

Āmār rakte niye āse tomār sur—
Jhaḍer ḍāk, banyār ḍāk, āguner ḍāk,
Pām̐jarer upare āchāḍ–khāoā
Maraṇ–sāgarer ḍāk,
Gharer śikal–nāḍā udāsī hāoār ḍāk.
Yena hām̐k diye āse
Apūrner sankīrṇa khāde
Pūrṇa sroter dākāti,
Chiniye nebe bhāsiye nebe bujhi.
Aṅge aṅge pak diye oṭhe
Kālbaiśākhīr ghurni–mār–khāoā
Araṇyer bakuni.

Ḍānā dey ni bidhātā,
Tomār gān diyeche āmār svapne
Jhoḍo ākāśe uḍo praṇer pāglāmi.
Ghare kāj kari śānta haye;
Sabāi bale 'bhālo'.
Tārā dekhe āmār icchār nei jor,
Sāṛā nei lobher,
Jhāpaṭ lāge māthār upar,
Dhuloy luṭoi māthā.
Duranta ṭhelāy niṣedher pāhārā kāt kare pheli

I don't know what you play
or what pain the tune evokes in whose mind.
Perhaps you play in cuckoo's note
the decline of the youthful south breeze.
While listening to it I think of myself
as a gently flowing stream at the feet of a mountain,
in whose heart has suddenly come
the rainy night of *Srabana.*
In the morning can be seen the banks flooded,
the unbearable swirl of water
pushing the stubborn stones.

Your tune brings in my blood
the rumble of storm, the surge of flood, the roar of fire,
the assault of the ocean of death
on the rib-cage,
the stirring of the door-chain by the listless wind.
It brings through the narrow channel of unfulfilment
the boom of high tide's plunder
as if to snatch and sweep me away.
Throughout my being coils up the agony
of a forest battered
by the whirlwind storm of *Baishakh.*

Providence did not give me wings,
but gave me your songs in my dreams—
the madness of a heart flying in a stormy sky.
I do my housework calmly
and everyone says, "Good."
They see that there is no strength in my will,
no response to my desires.
A gust of storm strikes my head
and it rolls in the dust.
I don't have the guts to even bend the barriers

Nei eman buker pāṭā;
Kaṭhin kare yāni ne bhālobāste,
Kāṁdte śudhu jāni,
Jāni eliye paṛte pāye.

Bāṁśioālā,
Beje oṭhe tomār bāṁśi,—
Ḍāk paḍe amartyaloke;
Sekhāne āpan garimāy
Upare uṭheche āmār māthā.
Sekhāne kuāśār pardā–cheṁḍā
Taruṇ surya āmār jīban.
Sekhāne āguner dānā mele dey
Āmār bāraṇ–na–mānā āgraha,
Uṛe cale ajānā śūnyapathe
Pratham–kṣudhāy–asthir garuṛer mato.
Jege oṭhe bidrohinī.
Tīksna cokher āṛe' jānāy ghṛṇā
Cār diker bhīrur bhiṛke,
Kriśa kuṭiler kāpuruṣatāke.

Bāṁśioālā,
Hayto āmāke dekhte ceyecha tumi.
Jāni ne, ṭhik jāygāṭi kothāy,
Ṭhik samay kakhan,
Cinbe keman kare.
Dosar–hārā āṣāḍher jhillijhanak rātre
Sei narī to chāyārupe
Geche tomār abhisāre cokh–eṛāno pathe.
Sei ajānāke kata basante
Pariyecha chāṁder mālā,
Śukobe nā tār phul.

of taboo with one unrestrained blow.
I don't know to love with all my might.
I know only to shed tears,
I know to submit at the feet.

O Flute-player,
your flute starts to play
and summons the heaven.
There my head, in its own pride,
rises high.
There my life is like the rising sun,
coming out tearing the curtain of fog.
There my fervour spreads its wings,
defying disapproval,
flies to the unknown emptiness
like Garuda bird fretful from its first hunger.
Awakens the rebel in me
and with piercing look shows revulsion
to the crowd of cowards around
and the impotence of the weak-
kneed hypocrites.

O Flute-player,
perhaps you wanted to meet me.
I don't know which is the right place,
when is the right time,
or how you will recognise me.
In a forlorn *Ashad* night filled with crickets' chirping,
that woman, like a shadow, has gone for her love-tryst
with you,
following the path hidden from the eyes.
You adorned that stranger
with garlands of rhythm in many springs.
Those flowers will never wither.

Tomār ḍāk śune ekdin
Gharpoṣā nirjīb meye
Andhakār kon theke
Beriye ela ghomṭā–khasā narī.
Yena se haṭhat–gāoā natun chanda Balmīkir,
Camak lāgālo tomākei.
Se nāmbe nā gāner āsan theke;
Se likhbe tomāke ciṭhi
Rāginīr ābchāyāy base.
Tumi jānbe nā tār ṭhikānā.

Ogo bāṁśoāla,
Se thāk tomār bāṁśir surer duratve.

✿✿✿✿✿

One day, hearing your summon,
the homebound lifeless girl
came out of her dark corner
as a woman casting away her veil.
As if she was a suddenly-sung new rhyme of *Valmiki*
and she amazed you.
She won't come down from her seat of singing.
She will write you letters
staying in shadow of your melodies.
You will not know her address.

Oh Flute-player,
let her stay at a distance in the melody of your flute.

❀❀❀❀❀

Ārogya (1941)

No. 23

Naṛī tumi dhanyā—
Āche ghar, āche gharkannā.
Tāri madhye rekhecha ektukhāni phaṁk.
Sethā hate paśe kāne bāhirer durbaler dāk.
Niye eso śuśruṣār dāli,
Sneha dāo dhāli.
Ȳe jībalakṣmīr pālaner śakti bahamān,
Narī tumi niyta śona tāhāri āhbān.
Sriṣṭibidhātār
Niyecha karmer bhār,
Tumi nārī
Tāṁhāri āpan sahakārī.
Unmukta karite thāka ārogyer path,
Nabīn karite thāka jirṇa ye jagat,
Śrīhārā ȳe tār 'pare tomār dhairyer sīmā nāi,
Āpan asādhya diye dayā taba tāniche tārāi.
Buddhibhraṣṭa asahiṣṇu apamān kare bāre bāre,
Cakṣu muche kṣamā karo tāre.
Akritagñatār dbāre āghāt sahicha dinrāti,
Lao śir pāti.
Ȳe abhāgā nāhi lāge kāje,
Praṇlakṣmī phele yāre ābarjanāmājhe,
Tumi tāre ānicha kuṛāye,
Tumi tāre ānicha kuṛāye,
Tār lañchanār tāp snigdha haste ditecha juṛāye.
Debatār ȳe pujā debār
Durbhāgāre kara dān sei mūlya tomār sebār.
Biśber pālanī śakti nijabīrȳe baha cupe cupe
Mādhurīr rūpe.
Bhraṣṭa ȳei bhagna ȳei, birūp bikrita,
Tāri lāgi sundarer hāter amrita.

❀❀❀❀❀

Recovery (1941)

No. 23

Woman, you are blessed.
you have your housework and your household.
Amidst that you have left a little crack
for the call of the weak of the world to buzz in your ear.
With your offering of nursing care
you shower them with affection and love.
At all times you hear the call
of the goddess of life's preservation.
The duty of the Creator
you bear on your shoulder.
You are woman,
you are his companion.
You keep on unbarring the door to recovery,
you renew all that is worn out and decrepit.
Limitless is your patience for the luckless,
their helplessness evokes your kindness.
The ignorant and the impatient insult you again and again.
Wiping your tears you shower them with forgiveness.
Ever aggrieved you are by ingratitude,
you bear it all with fortitude.
The hapless one who is of no use,
tossed by goddess of life in the refuse,
you gather him up with care
and with gentle touch you lighten his suffering's burden.
In your service you confer on the hapless
the same import as is in offerings to the gods.
Preserver of the world, with your own prowess
silently you bear it all as personified sweetness.
Those who are fallen, shattered, ugly and deformed
for them there is the solace of your benign hand.

Śeṣ Lekhan (1941)

No. 15

Tomār sṛṣtir path rekhecha ākīrṇa kari
Bicitra chalanājāle,
He chalanāmayī.
Mithyā biśbāser phāṁd petecha nipuṇ hāte
Saral jībane.
Ei prabañcanā diye mahattbere karecha ciṇhita;
Tār tare rākha ni gopan rātri.
Tomār jyotiṣka tāre
Ȳe–path dekhāy
Se ȳe tār antarer path,
Se ȳe cirasvaccha,
sahaj biśvāse se ye
Kare tāre cirasbamujjval.
Bahire kuṭil hok antare se riju,
Ei niye tāhār gourab.
Loke tāre bale biṛambita.
Satyere se pāy
Āpan āloke dhouta antare antare.
Kichute pāre nā tāre prabancite,
Śeṣ puraskār niye ȳāy se ȳe
Āpan bhāṇḍāre.
Anāyāse ȳe pereche chalanā sahite
Se pāy tomār hāte
Śantir akṣay adhikār.

Last Writing (1941)

No. 15

Strewn with a net of diverse deception
is the path of your creation,
O you enchantress!
With adept hands you've laid
the snare of false beliefs
in innocent lives.
With this deception you've marked the great;
for him you haven't left night's secret.
The course that your stars
show him
is his inner path,
ever transparent,
ever resplendent
by his simple faith.
However crafty outside, he is simple inside;
that's his pride.
Others say that he has been deceived.
In his heart truth he receives
bathed in his inner light.
Nothing can deceive him;
he takes his last reward
to his own storehouse.
Whoever can suffer your trickery at ease,
from your hands he receives
everlasting claim to peace.

✿✿✿✿✿

Citrangadā (1936)

I am Citrangada

Āmi Citrāngadā, rājendranandinī.
  Nahi debi, nahi sāmānyā nārī.
Pujā kari more rākhibe ūrdhe se nahi nahi,
Helā kari more rākhibe piche se nahi nahi.
Ȳadi parśe rākha more sankaṭe sampade,
Sammati dāo ȳadi kaṭhinabrate sahāy hate
  Pabe tabe tumi cinite more.
Āj śudhu kari nibedan—
Āmi Citrāngadā rājendranandinī.

Chitrangada (1936)

I am Chitrangada

I am Chitrangada, the daughter of a great king.
  I am neither a goddess nor an ordinary woman.
I am not to be worshipped on a pedestal
nor pushed behind in disrespect.
You will know me
if you keep me by your side in distress and in happiness.
Today I only say this —
  I am Chitrangada, the daughter of a great king.

Notes

Woman's Statement

Shephalika: also known as shephali and shiuli. A tree with small star-shaped flowers having orange-red stalks. They bloom mainly in autumn, opening at night and falling at dawn to form a white carpet under the tree. They have a sweet smell.

In the Night and in the Morning

Urbashi: A celestial nymph and a dancer in the court of Indra, the king of the gods. She is supposed to have unparallel beauty and eternal youth.

Churned sea: It is in Indian mythology that the ocean was churned at the beginning of creation by the gods and the demons, using Mandara mountain as the shaft and the giant serpent, Shessa, as the rope. Urbashi came out of the churned sea with a chalice of nectar in her right hand and a chalice of poison in her left hand.

Requital

Takshila: An ancient and powerful city of the Punjab, mentioned in Buddhist literature for its wealth and splemdor. Its site is now in Pakistan.

Kashi: Another name of the holy city of Benares.

Indra: mythological king of the gods.

Baruna: A river bordering Benares that joins the Ganges.

Ghat: A mooring place, a dock, a wharf or a staircase leading up to a pond or river where people can bathe or wash clothes.

Veena: A string instrument of the lute family. It is supposed to have been invented by Narada, chief of the Gandharvas or heavenly musicians. It is very much in use in India.

Sevenleafed tree: In Bengal it is also called *chatim.* It is a large evergreen tree with white flowers. Its name, *saptaparna,* implies that the leaves are in whorls of seven, but the number can vary.

Wild Geese, No. 23.

Churning of the ocean: See "In the Night and in the Morning."

Urbashi: See "In the night and in the Morning."

Lakshmi: the goddess of wealth, prosperity, luck and beauty, the consort of Vishnu, the second of the Hindu trinity.

Kingshuk: It can be called the "flame of the forest." It is a large tree with bright orange-red flowers like parrot's beak and without any scent. It flowers profusely in the spring and is associated with the spring festival.

Hemant: Late autumn season and' harvesting time, mid-October to mid-December.

Indelible Mark

Champak: an evergreen tree bearing very fragrant yellow-orange flowers.

Shaila: Literally meaning a stone. The poet uses it in the poem as a name for the girl and also to mean a 'burden' on her parents.

Mother was abashed: This phrase indicates that a male child is prefered over a female child.

Dada: elder brother or cousin. It is extended to other elder men out of affection or courtesy. It is also an affectionate term for addressing grandfather or a grandfather-like figure.

Emancipation

Veiling my face: the practice of married women partly covering their faces by pulling sari over their heads.

Lakshmi: See "Wild Geese, No.23."

Joint family: It refers to the practice of all brothers (with wife and children) living with parents under one roof and as one establishment sharing all income and expenses equally. The practice is on the decline.

Deliverance

Glory of his lineage: In the Hindu caste system there are sub-castes and heirarchies within the caste. In the Brahmin caste, highest of the four main castes, there are the *kulins,* highest of of the high. Panchanan belonged to the higher *kulin* sub-caste among the Brahmins.

Astabakra: A legendary sage whose body was crooked in eight different places due to a curse in his previous birth.

Yamadagna: A legendary sage and the father of Parasuram, one of the ten *Avatars* or incarnations of Vishnu according to the Hindu beliefs.

Baishakh: The first month of the Bengali calendar and the first month of summer, mid-April to mid-May.

Savitri: Refers to a story in the *Mahabharata* where Savitri, the daughter of King Ashvapati chose to marry the young and handsome Satyaban, the king of Salva. Narada told her that Satyaban was doomed to die in a few months. Satyaban died on the day he was predicted to die. As Yama, the god of death carried off Satyaban's soul, Savitri followed his steps until at last such fidelity and love touched the god of death. Yama promised to grant her wishes provided she would not ask to bring her husband back to life. "Then give me," Savitri said, "a hundred strong sons born of Satyaban to carry on our stock." Bound by his promise, the god of death had to bring the dead Satyaban back to life.

There is only one element in the story of Savitri that is common with the story of Manjulika. Her husband was also not expected to live long and he actually died within two months of Manjulika's marriage. Rabindranath ridicules Majulika's father's orthodox beliefs and caste pride by saying that the first part of the father's blessing, 'May you be like Savitri' came to be true, but not the second part.

Hookah: The Persian style water pipe for smoking tobacco, introduced in India during the Muslim rule. Now it it is rarely seen.

Luchi: Round flat bread made from bleached wheat flour and deep fried.

Day of austerity: Orthodox Hindus eat uncooked food, like fruits, yougurt, tapioka, etc. twice every month on the eleventh day of waxing and waning moon. Manjulika's father was conservative and orthodox in all other matters but his own food. Manjulika was forced to eat a strictly vegetarian diet, because she was a widow.

Paan-treat: Betel-leaf with betel-nut, shell-lime and spices for added taste are commonly chewed in India as chewing gums are in America.

When eleven months were to pass: It was the custom for a man to wait at least twelve months after his wife's death before he could re-marry.

Without a wife incomplete ....: A man is supposed to perform all riligious rituals with his wife by his side to earn merit. Since men wrote the rules this was the justification for widowers to remarry.

Manu: The founder of the solar race and the first law giver (codes of social and ethical rules of the Hindus).

The Mahabharata: One of the two epics of India, written by Vyasa.

The Strong

Seven Sages: The Indian name for the constellation, Great Bear or the Plough. Myth has it that the seven stars are the seven most renowned sages of ancient India.

Basket of Shredded Papers

Didi: elder sister, elder female cousins, and other elder women of the same generation and between grandparents and granddaughters.

Shahnai: a wind instrument like an oboe, often played at weddings and other ceremonies.

Ordinary Woman

Saratbabu: Refers to the great storyteller of Bengal, Saratchandra Chattopadhayay (1876-1937). See the introduction for more.

Bengali poet: Rabindranath is undoubtedly referring to himself. See introduction.

Seven goddesses: refers to the unfair battle of unequals in the Mahabharata where the boy Abhimanyu was slain by seven heroes. Here an ordinary woman has to compete with many extraordinary women.

Shakuntala: The heroine of the great drama, *Kalidasa,* by the foremost poet and dramatist in Sanskrit.

Not in the land of the ignorant: Rabindranath means Bengal here. It is perhaps a reference to the treatment he received from his detractors in Bengal who refused to recognise his genius until he was recognised in the West with the award of the Nobel Prize.

Modern Woman

Narad: A great sage of Indian mythology, the son of Brahma (the

Creator) and Saraswati (the goddess of learning). He was supremely skilled in music and poetry.

Kalidasa: Foremost poet and dramatist of Sanskrit literature of the fourth century.

Veena: See "Requital."

Rabi: Rabi literally means the sun. It is used here as a pun.

The Flute Player

Srabana: The forth month of the Bengali calendar and the second month of the monsoon season, from mid-July to mid-August.

Baishask: The first month of the Bengali calendar and the first month of summer, from mis-April to mid-may.

Garuda: A mythological bird, carrier of Vishnu, the protector of the creation.

Ashad: The third month of the Bengali calendar and the first month of the monsoon season, from mid-June to mid-July.

Valmiki: the supposed author of the epic *The Ramayana* in Sanskrit. He is also supposed to be the first poet.

I am Chitrangada

Chitrangada: The daughter of the king of Manipur in the *Mahabharata* epic. The mighty Arjuna married her.

Index

First line of poem in Bengali

First line of poem in English

Key to Transliteration

অ	আ [া]	ই [ি]	ঈ [ী]	উ [ু]	ঊ [ূ]	ঋ [ৃ]
a	ā	i	ī	u	ū	rh

এ [ে]	ঐ [ৈ]	ও [ো]	ঔ [ৌ]	ং	ঃ
e	oi	o	oū	ṅ	ḥ

ক	খ	গ	ঘ	ঙ	চ	ছ	জ	ঝ	ঞ	ট	ঠ	ড	ঢ
k	kh	g	gh	ng	c	ch	j	jh	ñ	ṭ	ṭh	ḍ	ḍh

ঢ়	ণ	ত	থ	দ	ধ	ন	প	ফ	ব	ভ	ম	য	য়
ḍh	ṇ	t	th	d	dh	n	p	ph	b	bh	m	ȳ	y

র	ল	শ	ষ	স	হ	ক্ষ	ঁ
r	l	ś	ṣ	s	ḥ	kṣ	ṁ